THE LITTLE BOOK OF CHOCOLATE

SWEET TREATS

To Marie and Milan, for their unfailing
support in my quest for the finest flavours.

THE LITTLE BOOK OF CHOCOLATE

SWEET TREATS

Make your own chocolates at home

MÉLANIE DUPUIS

Hardie Grant

BOOKS

CONTENTS

LIST OF RECIPES

HOW TO USE THIS BOOK

CHOCOLATE ESSENTIALS

Discover the main steps in chocolate-making. Essential skills
and basic recipes for making chocolates and pastries along with
infographics and explanations of specific preparation techniques.

RECIPES

Use chocolate-making techniques to create sweets, cakes and desserts. For each
recipe there are cross-references to the essentials, infographics to demonstrate
processes, and step-by step photos illustrating stages of composition.

ILLUSTRATED GLOSSARY

Helps with the finer details of how to use utensils. Illustrations
of techniques and skills for making chocolates and pastries.

CHAPTER 1

CHOCOLATE ESSENTIALS

THE CACAO POD

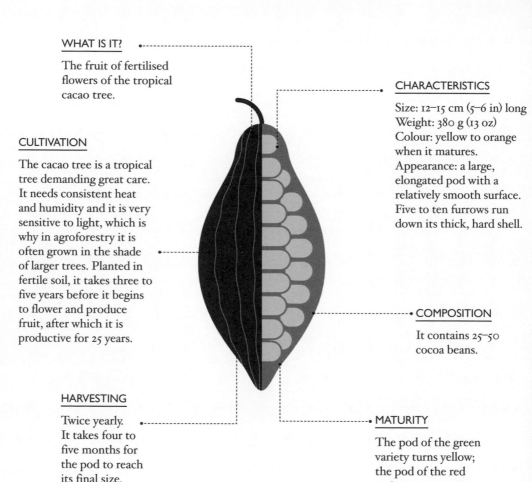

WHAT IS IT?

The fruit of fertilised flowers of the tropical cacao tree.

CULTIVATION

The cacao tree is a tropical tree demanding great care. It needs consistent heat and humidity and it is very sensitive to light, which is why in agroforestry it is often grown in the shade of larger trees. Planted in fertile soil, it takes three to five years before it begins to flower and produce fruit, after which it is productive for 25 years.

HARVESTING

Twice yearly. It takes four to five months for the pod to reach its final size.

CHARACTERISTICS

Size: 12–15 cm (5–6 in) long
Weight: 380 g (13 oz)
Colour: yellow to orange when it matures.
Appearance: a large, elongated pod with a relatively smooth surface. Five to ten furrows run down its thick, hard shell.

COMPOSITION

It contains 25–50 cocoa beans.

MATURITY

The pod of the green variety turns yellow; the pod of the red variety turns orange.

THE FRESH BEAN

WHAT IS IT?

The seed of the cacao tree, contained within the pod. The cocoa seed, or cocoa bean, is the seed after it has fermented.

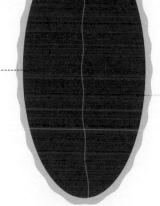

COMPOSITION

A fresh bean consists of an inner kernel covered with a light-coloured, acidic and sweet pulp and a thin but very tough, ribbed outer shell. So each bean consists of a shell and an inner kernel.

CHARACTERISTICS

Size: 2–3 cm (¾–1¼ in) long, 1–1.7 cm (½–¾ in) wide, 0.7–1.2 cm (½–¾ in) thick.
Colour: pink.

CHOCOLATE AROMA

The fresh bean has only a slight natural aroma. During fermentation and drying the aroma begins to develop. During roasting, the bean develops its final chocolate aroma.

HOW DOES THE CHOCOLATE FLAVOUR DEVELOP
DURING FERMENTATION AND ROASTING?

During the various stages of processing, a number of reactions take place, which lead to the formation of aromatic molecules, giving a variety of aromatic notes to the different chocolate varieties.

3 VARIETIES OF COCOA

FORESTARIO

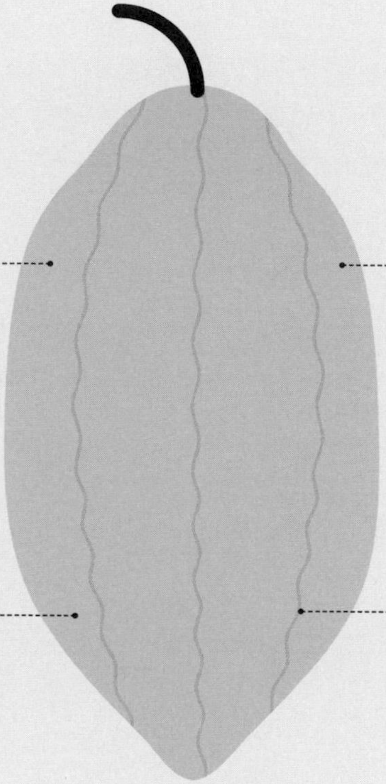

WHAT IS IT?

The world's most widely
cultivated variety of
cacao tree, accounting
for 80–90 per cent of
world production.

CHARACTERISTICS

A very resistant variety
with flowers that have
a violet pigmentation.
Pods: reddish-yellow,
of various shapes,
with a smooth surface
and rounded ends.
Beans: flattened.

ORIGINS

This variety originated
in the upper Amazon
and is found mainly
in South America.

FLAVOUR QUALITIES

Highly bitter, very
tannic and astringent.
Strongly aromatic.
The premium variety,
Nacional, is valued
for its finesse and
floral flavours.

CRIOLLO

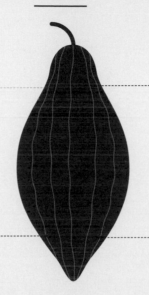

WHAT IS IT?

The finest and rarest variety of cacao tree, much appreciated by chocolate lovers. Production is less than 5 per cent of total world production.

ORIGINS

The very first cultivated variety of cacao tree (by the Maya in Venezuela, but it is also grown in Central America and Mexico). Its name (Spanish for 'creole') was given by settlers in Venezuela, a country that already had a reputation as a high-quality producer.

CHARACTERISTICS

This variety is particularly sensitive to disease and climatic variation. The pods are smooth and large, elongated, pointed, reddish and yellow. The beans are light-coloured and rounded with very little tannin.

TASTE QUALITIES

Low bitterness, highly aromatic, low in tannin and astringent. Very fine, delicate taste. The premium variety is Porcelana from Venezuela.

TRINITARIO

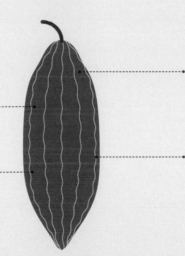

WHAT IS IT?

A cross of the Criollo and Forestario varieties. Cultivation of Trinitario represents 10–15 per cent of world production.

TASTE QUALITIES

With aromatic power and remarkable finesse, its qualities are somewhere between its parent varieties.

ORIGINS

Trinidad.

CHARACTERISTICS

The characteristics of the flowers, pods and beans are highly diverse and depend on the soil the tree is grown in.

FERMENTATION

WHAT IS FERMENTATION?

An operation carried out by the producer consisting of stopping the bean germination process in order to improve conservation and develop the aromas.

FERMENTATION

PERIOD

An average of 5–7 days.

FUNCTION

To remove the outer pulp of the cocoa beans, and prevent the germination of the beans, in order to add colour and aromatic notes.

METHODS

The length of fermentation varies according to variety, climate, volume of beans and the method. Beans can be stored:
- Method 1 (most common): in wooden crates that contain up to 80 kg (175 lb) of beans.
- Method 2: in baskets of woven plant fibres covered with banana leaves.
- Method 3: in heaps on banana leaves, which are folded over to completely cover the beans.

STAGES

Demucilage: sugars in the pulp are transformed into alcohol (alcoholic fermentation), which results in the production of heat, and the pulp breaks down into a liquid.
Brewing: the seeds are stirred for 2–8 days, depending on variety in order to accelerate the input of air and development of beneficial bacteria.
Airing: the beans are turned over and aired, promoting bacterial growth and stimulating aerobic fermentation. This converts alcohol into acetic acid, which is then absorbed by the beans, allowing enzymatic reactions to begin (acetic fermentation).

SPECIAL CARE

The planter must take special care to determine when fermentation should be stopped judging by the swelling of the beans, smell and other factors that have been learnt through observation and experience.

WHAT IS THE FUNCTION OF FERMENTATION?

Various chemical reactions take place during fermentation, allowing the outer pulp of the cocoa bean to be removed, preventing germination of the beans and bringing colour and aromatic notes to the beans.

THE BEANS

DRYING

WHAT IS IT?

The producer dries the cocoa beans in the sun after fermentation.

DURATION

8–15 days.

PRINCIPLE

After fermentation, the beans are left to dry in the sun on planks or racks and regularly turned over with a rake to ensure homogeneous drying and optimise subsequent conservation by stopping fermentation reactions. The moisture content reduces from 80 per cent to 5 per cent. The dried beans are then packed in jute bags.

CRUSHING

WHAT IS CRUSHING?

When the chocolate maker separates the cocoa bean from the shell.

PRINCIPLE

The dried beans are crushed coarsely in a mill to remove the inedible outer shell.

THE ROASTER

A constantly rotating drum used to roast cocoa. The regular movement of the drum allows the beans to be evenly roasted, without burning, in a process similar to that of roasting coffee beans.

ROASTING

WHAT IS ROASTING?

The chocolate maker roasts the cocoa beans to kill unwanted micro-organisms, reduce the water content (from 7 per cent to 2.5 per cent), improve separation between the shell and the kernel, eliminate mould and develop aromatic notes through various chemical reactions, including the Maillard reaction and caramelisation.

PRINCIPLE

Roasting temperature: 100–140°C (212–285°F) Roasting time: 15–40 minutes. When the beans reach 140°C (285°F), the Maillard reaction, which gives the chocolate its characteristic taste and aromas, occurs. The combined time and temperature variables will determine the main characteristics of the chocolate depending on the origin of the beans; their qualities, water content and size, and the type of chocolate being made.

GRINDING

WHAT IS GRINDING?

The grain of the cocoa bean is ground first into small fragments, or cocoa nibs, then further into a fine paste called cocoa mass.

PRINCIPLE

The cocoa beans pass through a grinder, then a milling machine. The resulting cocoa mass is mixed with the other raw materials (sugar, and sometimes milk) until a homogeneous paste is obtained. The granular size of the paste can be further reduced to between 20 and 25 microns using refining mills.

THREE GRINDING TECHNIQUES

Standard process

Roasted beans are hot-ground to produce coarse cocoa paste (also known as 'cocoa mass' or 'cocoa liquor').

More recent process

The beans are lightly moistened, then dried and shelled before being crushed to obtain small chips called 'green nibs'. These are roasted before being finely ground to produce cocoa mass or cocoa liquor.

Finer process

As above, the beans are lightly moistened, then dried and shelled before being crushed to obtain green nibs, which are first crushed, and then roasted. This method reduces the grain size to a level that the palate can hardly detect, resulting in a soft and silky texture in the mouth.

THE MACHINE

Milling machines grind the cocoa fragments and refine the paste. Two granite grindstones rotate on a base made of the same granite, crushing the cocoa paste over and over again to give a very fine texture of between 20 and 30 microns.

WHY IS THE FINENESS OF THE COCOA MASS IMPORTANT?

Grinding is a particularly critical step in the process as the fineness of the cocoa mass is an important characteristic that determines the quality of the chocolate.

CONCHING

WHAT IS CONCHING?

A mechanical process carried out by the chocolate maker, which gives the cocoa paste a smoother and silkier texture for a more refined taste. Conching also removes unpleasant volatile aromas, particularly acidity.

PRINCIPLE

The cocoa mass is poured into a large vat and stirred, backwards and forwards, with a roller, which moves in a similar way to a rolling pin. Under the granite slab at the base of the conching machine, heaters liquefy the chocolate, ensuring homogeneous conching. The more the chocolate is conched, the silkier and more intensely flavoured it becomes. Specialist chocolatiers conch their own chocolate for 72 hours to obtain the very best results.

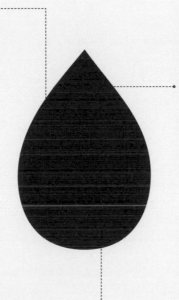

THE EQUIPMENT

The conching machine was invented in 1879 by the Swiss chocolatier Rodolphe Lindt. Today's models are very similar to the first machines and consist of a tank with a concave, granite bottom that is heated from beneath. The continuous conching process is now done with a metal roller.

HOW DOES THE CHANGE IN TEXTURE COME ABOUT?

During conching, the sharp edges of the cocoa particles are worn away. The rounded particles improve the fluidity of the chocolate, which becomes smooth and shiny. Cocoa butter is also released, bringing velvety smoothness.

COCOA MASS

COCOA MASS

WHAT IS COCOA MASS?

It is the substance obtained after grinding the beans, also called cocoa liquor or cocoa paste. The chocolate maker will add other ingredients (sugar, vanilla, etc.) to make chocolate.

FUNCTION

It gives chocolate its aromatic qualities and characteristic taste.

COCOA POWDER

WHAT IS COCOA (UNSWEETENED CHOCOLATE) POWDER?

Powder obtained after grinding the kernels of fermented cocoa beans from the cacao tree. It is extremely fine and has a low fat content. It is produced in a press, and the residue of the pressing is a very compact cake several centimetres (1–2 in) thick containing only 10–20 per cent fat. Crushed, then finely pulverised, it becomes cocoa powder.

FUNCTION

Cocoa powder is a basic ingredient for all chocolate flavourings: biscuits, ice creams, dairy products, confectionery, etc. It is also a raw material for making spreads.

WHAT ARE THE DESIRED QUALITIES OF COCOA POWDER?

Cocoa powder must have good colouring properties, provide the desired flavouring (depending on the beans and the roasting process) and be very finely ground.

WHAT DOES THE PERCENTAGE OF COCOA MEAN?

It shows the total amount of cocoa bean in the chocolate. A 70 per cent cocoa chocolate is 70 per cent cocoa mass and 30 per cent sugar.

DISCOVERING THE ART OF COCOA BUTTER

WHAT IS IT USED FOR?

Cocoa butter strongly influences the final texture of the chocolate. Its content varies greatly from one recipe to another.

WHAT TYPE SHOULD I CHOOSE?

Using cocoa butter chips makes weighing and melting easier.

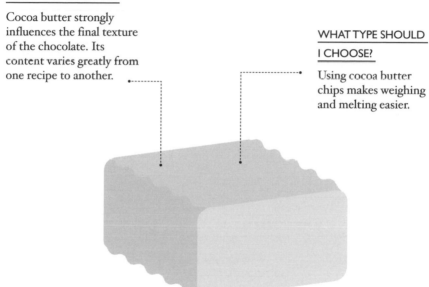

WHAT HAPPENS WHEN COCOA BUTTER MELTS?

Solid cocoa butter is made up of different kinds of crystals, which each melt at different temperatures. When tempering the chocolate, the chocolate maker carefully heats it to a temperature that preserves the desired crystals and makes the others disappear.

SUGAR

WHICH SUGAR SHOULD I CHOOSE?

Cane sugar: neutral taste (most chocolate).
Coconut sugar: neutral taste, low glycaemic index.
Lucuma powder: neutral taste, low glycaemic index.

WHAT IS SUGAR?

A product extracted from sugar cane or sugar beet.

FUNCTION

It is the third main ingredient in chocolate. It reduces bitterness, enhances the powerful natural flavour of the beans and turns it into a delicacy.

VANILLA & MILK

VANILLA

WHAT IS VANILLA?

Vanilla is a standard ingredient in most white chocolate.

FUNCTION

Vanilla is used to flavour and mellow the taste in chocolate recipes. Though it is a standard ingredient, it is not always included. For example, it is not present in dark chocolate.

MILK

WHAT SORT OF MILK IS USED?

Usually cow's milk. Fresh milk, milk powder, concentrated milk and sweetened condensed milk may also be used.

FUNCTION

An essential ingredient in milk chocolate and white chocolate, it makes the chocolate smoother and mellower.

DARK CHOCOLATE

COMPOSITION

Dark or plain (baking, bittersweet or semi-sweet) chocolate must contain at least 35 per cent cocoa.

ENERGY

Three squares, or 30 g (about 1 oz) of 70 per cent cocoa dark chocolate provide: 160 calories, 12 g of fat (7 g of which are saturated), 8 g of sugar and 2–4 g of fibre. Three squares of 85 per cent cocoa dark chocolate provide the same number of calories (160), more fat (14 g), less sugar (4 g) and 2–4 g of fibre.

TASTE

Chocolate with less than 65 per cent cocoa has a sweet flavour and is often used in dessert chocolates for pastries. Chocolate with 65 per cent or 70 per cent cocoa is more bitter. It is used in cooking (baking chocolate) or for eating in bars. Chocolate with 80 per cent cocoa is much stronger in character. More bitter, it has a less of a melt-in-the-mouth texture. Chocolate with 90 per cent or more cocoa is very bitter, to be enjoyed in very small quantities.

IS THE PERCENTAGE OF COCOA SYNONYMOUS WITH QUALITY?

No – quality is determined by other factors, above all by the variety of beans and the care taken during the processing stages. More chocolate makers are becoming more transparent about their processes and ingredients.

WHY DOES CHOCOLATE'S SURFACE TURN WHITE?

Chocolate contains fat crystals, some of which, over time, rise to the surface resulting in what's known as 'bloom'.

MILK & WHITE CHOCOLATE

MILK CHOCOLATE

COMPOSITION

Good-quality milk chocolate contains between 25 per cent and 40 per cent cocoa. It has less fat than dark chocolate but more sugar.

TASTE

A quality milk chocolate is a beautiful light brown. It should break with a 'snap' and melt in the mouth. Milk makes it smooth and sugar gives it a rounded flavour.

WHITE CHOCOLATE

COMPOSITION

It doesn't contain cocoa solids, but does contain cocoa butter, milk or milk powder and sugar, and often vanilla.

TASTE

Creamy and sweet, and often vanilla.

WHY ARE MILK AND WHITE CHOCOLATE SOFTER THAN DARK CHOCOLATE?

White and milk chocolates contain more cocoa butter, giving them softer textures. Dark chocolate contains less cocoa butter making it more brittle.

TEMPERING

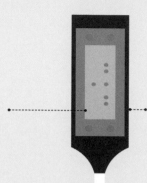

WHAT IS TEMPERING?

Also called 'pre-crystallisation', tempering means subjecting the chocolate to a temperature curve so that it can be melted and worked on while retaining its taste and visual qualities. Use good-quality chocolate with at least 32 per cent cocoa butter for tempering, ideally 'couverture'.

DARK COUVERTURE CHOCOLATE
1. Melts between 55° (131°F) and 58°C (136.5°F)
2. Lower the temperature to between 28° (82.4°F) and 29°C (84.2°F)
3. Increase the temperature to between 31° (87.8°F) and 32°C (89.6°F)

MILK COUVERTURE CHOCOLATE
1. Melts between 45° (113°F) and 48°C (118.4°F)
2. Lower the temperature to between 27° (80.6°F) and 28°C (82.4°F)
3. Increase the temperature to between 29° (84.2°F) and 30°C (86°F)

WHITE COUVERTURE CHOCOLATE
1. Melts between 45° (113°F) and 48°C (118.4°F)
2. Lower the temperature to between 26° (78.8°F) and 27°C (80.6°F)
3. Increase the temperature to between 28° (82.4°F) and 29°C (84.2°F)

WHAT IS THE PURPOSE OF TEMPERING?

It allows the chocolate to retain its crunchiness, brittleness and ability to melt and to have a silky, shiny appearance. When correctly tempered, chocolate is more stable and less sensitive to moisture and heat.

WHAT HAPPENS DURING TEMPERING?

The chocolate mass is seeded with microcrystals. After melting, the chocolate is cooled to allow stable and unstable microcrystals to form. Then, by bringing the temperature back up, the unstable microcrystals are removed and only stable crystals remain.

PREPARE YOUR EQUIPMENT

Wipe the work surface clean
with a moist cloth and cover with
cling film (plastic wrap), which
will then stick to the surface.
This makes cleaning up easy: just
peel away the film. Place a cloth
near the double-boiler to prevent
water splashing onto the work
surface when taking the bowl out
of the boiler. Placing the bowl
of chocolate on a non-slip ring
makes it more stable as you work
and allows it to cool more slowly.

MELTING

Increasing the temperature
makes all the fat molecules melt.

LOWERING THE TEMPERATURE

Once the couverture chocolate
has reached its melting
temperature (depending on
the type of chocolate; see
opposite), let the bowl cool
down at room temperature
until it reaches its working
temperature. The easiest way is
just to let the melted couverture
stand until it cools down to
the required temperature.

You can speed up the process by
placing the bowl in a cold-water
bath, making sure that the water
outside the bowl reaches the top
level of the chocolate. Mix it
regularly with a spatula to keep it
at a constant temperature.

Be careful not to splash water
into the chocolate during mixing.

INCREASING THE TEMPERATURE

Bring the chocolate up to
working temperature on the hot
water double-boiler (page 118).

USING THE MELTED CHOCOLATE AND KEEPING IT AT THE RIGHT TEMPERATURE

Regularly check the temperature
of the chocolate: when it goes
down more than 2°C (3.6°F)
below its working temperature,
bring the temperature back up
on the double-boiler heating it
in 10-second stages, but being
careful not to overheat it.

MELTING

WHAT IS IT?

Transforming solid
chocolate (in pieces)
into liquid.

EQUIPMENT YOU WILL NEED

Cutting board
Serrated knife
Double-boiler
Microwavable mixing bowl

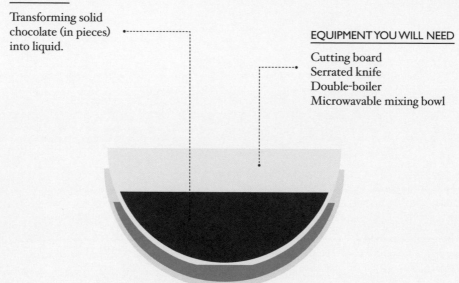

TIP

When melting in a double-
boiler, make sure the bowl
containing the chocolate
does not touch the bottom of
the pan or the surface of the
water, or the chocolate may
overheat or burn. It is the
steam that melts the chocolate,
not a direct heat source.
Chop the chocolate into
regular-sized pieces or use
good-quality chocolate chips.

HOW TO DO IT

In a double-boiler (page
118): half fill a saucepan with
hot water, put the chocolate
in a bowl and place it on
the saucepan above the hot
water. Let the chocolate
melt slowly, stirring with
a spatula until a smooth,
even texture is reached.

In the microwave: put the
chocolate in a microwave-safe
(non-metallic) double-boiler.
Heat for 1 minute at 500 W,
then stir with a spatula. Repeat
the operation in 30-second
stages, stirring each time.
Check the temperature
(depending on the chocolate
you are making, see page 24).

TEMPERING METHOD 1:
THE KITCHEN WORKTOP METHOD

WHAT IS IT?

The classic method for bringing chocolate to its optimum working temperature after melting.

ADVANTAGE

This technique is used by professional chocolatiers. It produces very stable results.

EQUIPMENT YOU WILL NEED

Unrefrigerated marble surface
Mixing bowl
Double boiler
Thermometer
Triangle
Palette knife

DISADVANTAGE

Requires space and equipment.

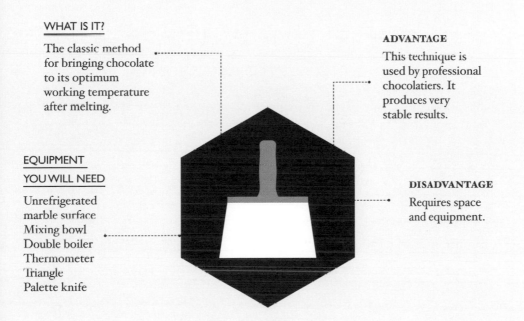

ADVICE

Avoid stainless steel worktops, which retain too much heat. Also avoid working on refrigerated marble, which is extremely moist and too cold, and will cause the chocolate to thicken irreversibly. Once the couverture chocolate has melted, pour out three quarters of it onto the worktop.

Spread the chocolate on the worktop and mix by folding it back on itself using a triangle and a palette knife. The temperature must remain constant depending on the chocolate you are making (see page 24), so you should check it regularly with a thermometer.

Put half of the warm couverture chocolate back into the double-boiler bowl to halt the cooling process immediately and mix well. Gradually add the rest of the hot couverture until it reaches its correct optimum working temperature (see page 24).

TEMPERING METHOD 2:
THE SEEDING METHOD

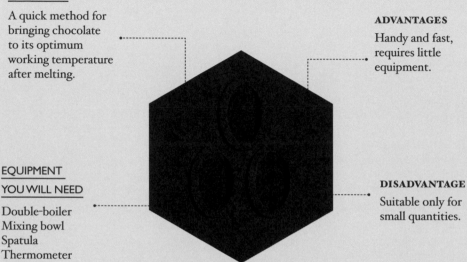

WHAT IS IT?

A quick method for bringing chocolate to its optimum working temperature after melting.

ADVANTAGES

Handy and fast, requires little equipment.

EQUIPMENT
YOU WILL NEED

Double-boiler
Mixing bowl
Spatula
Thermometer

DISADVANTAGE

Suitable only for small quantities.

HOW TO DO IT

When the couverture chocolate has melted, add 30 per cent of the chocolate chips using a spatula. Stir continuously to produce the seeding effect and to ensure a constant temperature, depending on the chocolate you are making (see page 24). Check the temperature and gradually add more chocolate chips until the working temperature is reached depending on the chocolate you are making (see page 24).

WHAT DOES 'SEEDING' MEAN?

Using the properties of the stable cocoa butter molecules in the chocolate chips to seed other molecules and make them stable. Unstable crystals tend to align themselves to the stable crystals as if by imitation.

TEMPERING METHOD 3:
LEAVING TO STAND

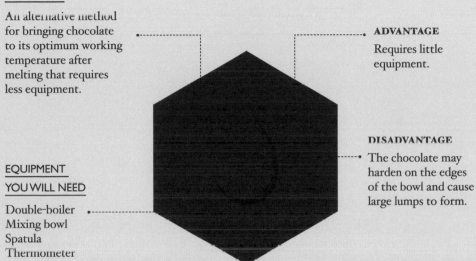

An alternative method
for bringing chocolate
to its optimum working
temperature after
melting that requires
less equipment.

ADVANTAGE

Requires little
equipment.

DISADVANTAGE

The chocolate may
harden on the edges
of the bowl and cause
large lumps to form.

EQUIPMENT
YOU WILL NEED

Double-boiler
Mixing bowl
Spatula
Thermometer

HOW TO DO IT

When the couverture chocolate
has reached its melting
temperature (depending on the
chocolate you are making, see
page 24), at room temperature,
let the bowl cool down until
the chocolate reaches its
working temperature.

You can speed up the process
by placing the bowl in a
cold-water bath, making
sure that the water in the
outer bowl reaches the top
level of the chocolate in the
inner bowl. Mix regularly
with a spatula to maintain
a constant temperature.

Take care not to splash water
into the chocolate during
mixing. To do this, stabilise
the base of the bowl by
placing a non-slip ring under
the bowl containing the cold
water. Then bring it back up
to working temperature on
a hot water double-boiler.

TEMPERING METHOD 4:
USING MYCRYO COCOA BUTTER POWDER

WHAT IS IT?

An easy method for bringing chocolate to its optimum working temperature after melting that's ideal for small quantities.

EQUIPMENT
YOU WILL NEED

Double boiler
Mixing bowl
Spatula
Thermometer

TYPICAL USE

Decoration for which a very small quantity is needed (for example, the wings and eyes of a chocolate hen).

ADVANTAGE

Allows small quantities to be prepared quickly.

DISADVANTAGES

Suitable only for small quantities. Shorter shelf life: chocolate may develop a white 'bloom' more quickly.

ADVICE

If you have no Mycryo, chop up pure cocoa butter very finely.

HOW TO DO IT

Start by melting the couverture chocolate in a double-boiler. When about 90 per cent of the chocolate chips have melted, remove from the heat. The couverture will be at around 40°C (104°F). Stir in the remaining chips until melted completely, and the couverture is at around 35°C (95°F). Gently fold in the Mycryo with a spatula. Allow the temperature to drop to working temperature, depending on the chocolate selected (see page 24).

WHAT IS THE FUNCTION
OF MYCRYO

Mycryo, a brand of powdered cocoa butter, is used to seed the chocolate. It provides stable crystals that seed the tempering process.

KEEPING CHOCOLATE AT THE RIGHT WORKING TEMPERATURE

WHAT IS IT?

Three ways to keep couverture chocolate at the right working temperature or reheat for use.

EQUIPMENT YOU WILL NEED

Double boiler
Mixing bowl
Saucepan
Thermometer

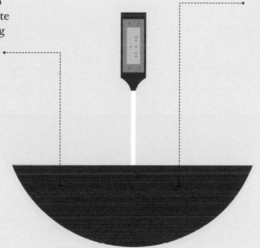

TIPS

If the correct working temperature is exceeded, you should go back to the beginning and repeat the tempering process.

Method 1: Heat in a double-boiler bowl, removing it regularly from the heat to check the temperature depending on the chocolate you have chosen (see page 24). Care must be taken as the bowl keeps its heat and transfers it to the chocolate even when it is out of the hot water.

Method 2: keep some couverture warm and add it to the cooled chocolate in order to reheat it.

Method 3: use a professional tempering machine, these are designed to keep couverture chocolate at just the right temperature.

COATING CHOCOLATES

WHAT DOES IT MEAN?

Giving chocolates a fine, crisp outer coating.

TRICKY POINT

Tempering the couverture chocolate.

HOW LONG WILL IT TAKE?

Preparation: 2 hours
Leave to stand:
12 hours (ganache),
48 hours (setting)

SKILLS REQUIRED

Tempering chocolate
(page 24)
Coating with a thin
layer of chocolate
(chabloning; page 115)
Removing the baking
frame (page 115)

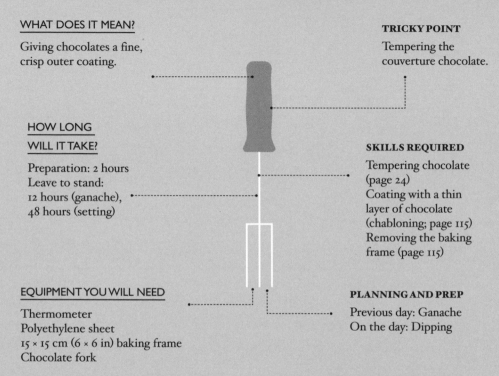

EQUIPMENT YOU WILL NEED

Thermometer
Polyethylene sheet
15 × 15 cm (6 × 6 in) baking frame
Chocolate fork

PLANNING AND PREP

Previous day: Ganache
On the day: Dipping

TIP

When all the sweets have been dipped, pour the remaining chocolate onto a baking sheet, let it harden and keep in a dry place. Use it to make chocolate mousse, ganache or fondants. Do not re-temper, as the chocolate will lose its fluidity. Covering the underside and top of the ganache with a fine layer of chocolate first (chabloning; page 115) makes it easier to handle during coating.

WHY DOESN'T THE GANACHE MELT WHEN IT IS DIPPED IN COUVERTURE CHOCOLATE?

The ganache is at 17°C (62.6°F) when it is immersed in the 28–35°C (82.4–95°F) couverture. This temperature difference means that the ganache does not melt or only does so slightly, on the surface.

METHOD

1. Temper 200 g (7 oz) of couverture chocolate (page 24). Put a polyethylene sheet on a baking tray and coat with a thin layer of tempered chocolate using a brush (page 115), then put the frame on the sheet.

2. To make the ganache, pour it into the frame when it is at the right temperature: 35°C (95°F) for dark chocolate, 32°C (89.6°F) for milk chocolate and 27–28°C (80.6–82.4°F) for white. Smooth it out, then leave to set for 10–12 hours at 15–17°C (59–62.6°F).

3. Temper the remaining couverture. Remove the frame (page 115). Coat the top surface with a thin layer of chocolate (page 115) using a spatula. Before the thin chocolate layer has cooled completely, cut the sweets to size using a knife.

4. To coat in the couverture chocolate: using a chocolate fork, dip it into the melted chocolate, moving it up and down. Lift it out: the melted chocolate should stick to the outside but should not run off when it is put on a polyethylene sheet. Leave to sit at 15–17°C (59–62.6°F) for 48 hours to ensure the cocoa fat has fully set.

MAKING MOULDED CHOCOLATES

WHAT DOES IT MEAN?

Using a mould to
make beautifully
shaped chocolates.

TRICKY POINT

Tempering the
chocolate.

**HOW LONG
WILL IT TAKE?**

Preparation: 2 hours
Leave to stand:
12 hours (ganache)
48 hours (setting
once sealed)

SKILLS REQUIRED

Tempering
chocolate (page 24)
Using a piping
bag (page 120)

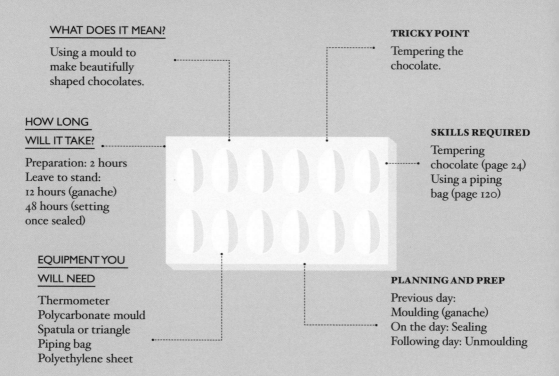

**EQUIPMENT YOU
WILL NEED**

Thermometer
Polycarbonate mould
Spatula or triangle
Piping bag
Polyethylene sheet

PLANNING AND PREP

Previous day:
Moulding (ganache)
On the day: Sealing
Following day: Unmoulding

ADVICE

Make sure that the moulds are
clean and wipe the imprints
carefully with cotton wool to
remove any trace of moisture
or grease. Be careful not to
leave any fingermarks. When
handling the mould, hold it by
its edges and avoid prolonged
hand contact with the mould
imprints, as body heat is higher
than the temperature at which
the couverture chocolate is
used and white marks ('bloom')
may appear after crystallisation.
Do not wait too long between
layers so that they adhere
well to each other and do
not separate on eating.

TIPS

Spray the first layer into the
moulds with a chocolate
spray gun, if you have one.
Ideally leave to stand for 48
hours, but the chocolates can
be unmoulded in four to six
hours. If unmoulding is not
going well, place the mould in
the freezer for 15 minutes.

1. Temper two-thirds of the coating chocolate (page 24). Apply a thin layer in the mould using a dry brush. Wait a few minutes for this first coat to begin to set.

2. Fill the mould imprints completely using a ladle. Tap on the side of the mould with the handle of a spatula to allow air bubbles to escape.

3. Turn the mould over and tap to remove excess chocolate.

Leave the mould upside-down and place it on spacers so that the excess chocolate runs out.

4. When the couverture begins to set, scrape the mould with a triangle or spatula. If the previous coat is too thin, apply a second coat, following steps 2 and 3. Allow to set for about 2 hours. During that time, make the soft or semi-liquid filling and allow it to cool down to a temperature of 27°C (80.6°F). Using a piping

bag (page 120) fill the moulds stopping 2–3 mm from the top. Leave to set for 10–12 hours at 15–17°C (59–62.6°F).

5. When the chocolates have set, temper the rest of the couverture to seal the sweets: fill the remaining space in each mould, pat, scrape and put on a polyethylene sheet.

6. To unmould the chocolates, twist the mould slightly, turn it over and tap on the side.

DECORATING CHOCOLATES

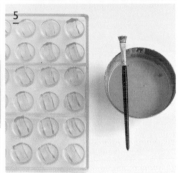

1 FORK

After coating, place the chocolate on a polyethylene sheet and immediately use the prongs of a fork to trace a decoration on the surface. Then lift off the fork and leave to set.

2 CONE

When the chocolate has set, fill a cone (page 116) with melted couverture and, working quickly, run fine threads of chocolate onto the surface. Leave the decoration to set.

3 TOPPING

After coating, put a few crushed seeds or nuts on the surface and leave to set.

4 GOLD LEAF

After coating, add a fragment of gold leaf using a toothpick and allow to set.

5 PAINTBRUSH DECORATION

Prepare a decorating paste of 70 g (2½ oz) white couverture chocolate, 10 g (½ oz) cocoa butter and a very small amount of fat-soluble food colouring. Brush each mould imprint with the paste before coating it with chocolate.

DECORATING CHOCOLATE

1 FLAKES

Temper 150 g (5 oz) couverture chocolate (page 24), pour onto the back of a baking tray and spread out a thin layer using a palette knife. Wait a few minutes for the chocolate to begin to set, then using a dessert ring or a pastry cutter, scrape off flakes of chocolate.

2 CHOCOLATE DISCS

Temper 150 g (5 oz) couverture chocolate (page 24), pour onto a polyethylene sheet and spread out a thin layer using a palette knife. Wait a few minutes for the chocolate to begin to set, then using pastry rings or cutters, cut out discs. Place a baking sheet and a tray on top to prevent them from curling as they set and the couverture shrinks.

3 CHOCOLATE SQUARES

Temper 150 g (5 oz) couverture chocolate (page 24), pour onto a polyethylene sheet and spread out a thin layer using a palette knife. Wait a few minutes for the chocolate to begin to set, then using a ruler and a paring knife, cut 3 cm (1¼ in) strips crosswise and lengthwise to make squares. Place a baking sheet and a tray on top to prevent them from curling as they set and the couverture shrinks.

4 COCOA NIB DISCS

Temper 150 g (5 oz) couverture chocolate (page 24), pour onto a polyethylene sheet and spread out a thin layer using a palette knife. Sprinkle with cocoa nibs. Wait a few minutes for the chocolate to begin to set, then using dessert rings or pastry cutters, cut out discs. You can also put the couverture in a piping bag (page 120) and pipe out discs on a polyethylene sheet. Tap on the sheet so that the chocolate evenly spreads out.

5 DECORATIVE CAKE SURROUND

Put a baking tray in the freezer for 30 minutes. Melt the chocolate in a double-boiler at about 40°C (104°F). Remove the baking tray from the freezer and quickly spread out a thin layer of chocolate using a palette knife. Using a ruler and a paring knife, cut a strip of chocolate to the required size. Gently peel the strip off the tray with the knife and put it immediately around the cake.

DECORATING CHOCOLATE

6 LATTICE EFFECT DECORATIONS

Temper 150 g (5 oz) couverture chocolate (page 24), put it in a piping bag, make a very small hole in the bag, then pipe out thin, overlapping hoops onto a polyethylene sheet (page 120). Leave to set, then break off to make decorative pieces.

7 CIGARETTE SHAPES AND MINIATURE FANS

Temper 150 g (5 oz) couverture chocolate (page 24), pour onto the back of a baking tray and spread out a thin layer using a palette knife. Wait a few minutes for the chocolate to begin to set, then using a triangle, scrape 2–3 cm (1 in) to roll into cigarette shapes. Slightly change the angle to produce small fans.

For flakes, score the surface in one direction across the width of a strip, then scrape off.

8 CHOCOLATE SWIRLS

Temper 150 g (5 oz) couverture chocolate (page 24), pour onto a polyethylene sheet and spread out a thin layer using a palette knife. Holding the top end of the sheet, pull a chocolate comb towards you to score lines on the chocolate. Now twist the strip into a swirl shape, put a weight on each end so the strip does not unroll, and leave to set.

9 WOLF FANGS

Temper 150g (5 oz) couverture chocolate, pour onto a polyethylene sheet and spread out a thin layer using a palette knife. Wait a few minutes for the chocolate to begin to set then, using a ruler and a paring knife, cut 8 cm (3¼ in) wide and 3 cm (1¼ in) long strips to make rectangles, then cut diagonally to make triangles. Put a baking sheet and a tray on top to prevent them from curling up as they set and the couverture shrinks.

10 CHOCOLATE FEATHERS

Temper 150 g (5 oz) couverture chocolate (page 24), dip the blade of a paring knife into the chocolate and place the chocolate-filled blade on a strip of polyethylene sheet or transparent acetate strip. Lift the blade of the knife up slightly and pull it towards you to produce a feather. Put in a round mould to shape the decorations.

50% PRALINE & GIANDUJA

WHAT IS IT?

Praline is a soft paste made of 50 per cent nuts and 50 per cent sugar. Chocolate is added to make gianduja.

HOW LONG WILL IT TAKE?

Preparation:
30 minutes
Standing:
2 hours

EQUIPMENT YOU WILL NEED

Thermometer
Food processor for cutting and blending

WHAT IS IT USED FOR?

Flavouring for Paris-Brest cakes; fillings for chocolate sweets.

WHY ARE THE NUTS ROASTED?

Roasting reduces the water content and develops the aromas.

VARIATIONS

Increase the proportion of nuts by reducing the amount of sugar (70 per cent nuts and 30 per cent sugar for example). Use only hazelnuts and almonds to make praline.

TRICKY POINTS

Caramelising nuts
Crushing praline nuts

STORING

Several weeks in an airtight box in a dry place.

ADVICE

Process in small quantities if needed, depending on the how powerful the mixer is. If the mixture starts to get hot, stop and wait a few minutes. To prevent the sugar from burning during caramelisation, remove the pan from the heat from time to time and mix well.

TIPS

Make sure that the nuts are fresh so that the praline can be kept for some time without going rancid.
To check if the nuts are cooked, cut one in half: it should be a golden colour inside.

FOR 600 G (1 LB 5 OZ) PRALINE

150 g (5 oz) shelled almonds
150 g (5 oz) shelled hazelnuts
120 g (4 oz) water
300 g (10½ oz) white
caster (superfine) sugar

FOR 320 G (11 OZ) GIANDUJA

120 g (4 oz) dark couverture
chocolate (66% cocoa)
200 g (7 oz) praline

FOR THE PRALINE

1. Preheat the oven to 170°C
(340°F/gas 5). Put the almonds
and hazelnuts on a tray lined

with baking parchment and
bake for 15–20 minutes.

2. Put the water, then sugar in a
saucepan. Bring to the boil over
a medium–high heat, then put
the thermometer in the mixture,
taking care not to let it touch
the bottom or sides of the pan.
Heat until it is 110°C (230°F).

3. Remove from the heat
and add the roasted nuts.
Stir with a spatula until the
sugar crystallises. Return
to medium heat and then,
stirring continuously,
cook until the white sugar
caramelises around the nuts.

4. Transfer immediately to a
baking tray lined with baking
parchment (lay it as flat as
possible) and leave to cool to
room temperature. Coarsely
crush, then put in a food
processor fitted with a blade
and blend until smooth. Put
aside in an airtight tin.

FOR THE GIANDUJA

1. Melt the chocolate in a
double-boiler (page 118).

2. Mix it with the praline. Use
immediately or spread on a sheet
and leave to harden for later use.

CREAMY GANACHE

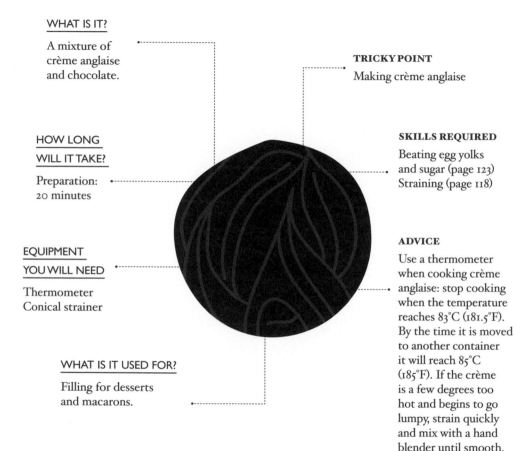

WHAT IS IT?

A mixture of
crème anglaise
and chocolate.

HOW LONG
WILL IT TAKE?

Preparation:
20 minutes

EQUIPMENT
YOU WILL NEED

Thermometer
Conical strainer

WHAT IS IT USED FOR?

Filling for desserts
and macarons.

TRICKY POINT

Making crème anglaise

SKILLS REQUIRED

Beating egg yolks
and sugar (page 123)
Straining (page 118)

ADVICE

Use a thermometer
when cooking crème
anglaise: stop cooking
when the temperature
reaches 83°C (181.5°F).
By the time it is moved
to another container
it will reach 85°C
(185°F). If the crème
is a few degrees too
hot and begins to go
lumpy, strain quickly
and mix with a hand
blender until smooth.

WHY IS CRÈME ANGLAISE LIKELY TO
GO LUMPY IF IT OVERHEATS?

*Crème anglaise contains egg protein. If overheated, the
proteins coagulate and give the crème a lumpy texture.*

FOR 450 G (1 LB) GANACHE

50 g (2 oz) egg yolk (3 or 4 yolks)
50 g (2 oz) white caster
(superfine) sugar
250 g (9 oz) milk
150 g (5 oz) plain, dark chocolate
60% cocoa (minimum)

1. Beat the yolks with
the sugar (page 123).

2. Bring the milk almost to
the boil. Just before it boils,
pour half of it onto the egg
yolk and sugar mixture. Mix
with a whisk. When the
mixture is evenly blended,
pour back into the saucepan.

3. Return to a medium heat,
stirring all the time with a
spatula, until a thin layer of
cream coats the spatula when
it is removed (85°C/185°F).

4. Take off the boil, immediately
add the chocolate, mix together
and blend. Strain the mixture
(page 118). Cover with cling
film (plastic wrap). Keep
refrigerated until ready to use.

WHIPPED WHITE GANACHE

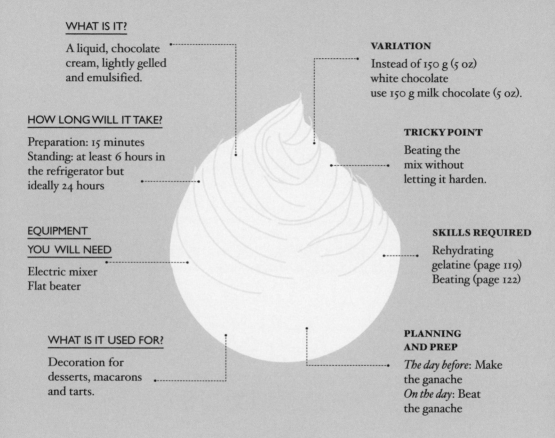

WHAT IS IT?

A liquid, chocolate cream, lightly gelled and emulsified.

HOW LONG WILL IT TAKE?

Preparation: 15 minutes
Standing: at least 6 hours in the refrigerator but ideally 24 hours

EQUIPMENT
YOU WILL NEED

Electric mixer
Flat beater

WHAT IS IT USED FOR?

Decoration for desserts, macarons and tarts.

VARIATION

Instead of 150 g (5 oz) white chocolate use 150 g milk chocolate (5 oz).

TRICKY POINT

Beating the mix without letting it harden.

SKILLS REQUIRED

Rehydrating gelatine (page 119)
Beating (page 122)

PLANNING AND PREP

The day before: Make the ganache
On the day: Beat the ganache

WHAT HAPPENS WHEN GANACHE HARDENS?

If the ganache has not cooled enough before whipping, it may heat up in the mixer and the gelatine will melt. As it melts, the gelatine will become unstable and the ganache will harden.

WHY DOES GANACHE BECOME MATT AFTER WHIPPING?

Ganache becomes matt for two reasons: the white chocolate crystallises and air is incorporated into the ganache.

FOR 350 G (12 OZ) GANACHE

2 g (1 sheet) sheet gelatine
230 g (8 oz) whipping cream
150 g (5 oz) white chocolate

1. Rehydrate the gelatine (page 119) in cold water.

2. Heat the cream until it begins to boil. Remove from the heat and add the gelatine. Mix, then pour over the white chocolate in a heatproof bowl. Wait 1 minute, then whisk. Pour into a bowl or container, cover with cling film (plastic wrap) and leave to chill in the refrigerator for at least 6 hours, ideally overnight.

3. Put the cold ganache into a stand mixer fitted with a flat whisk attachment (see above) and beat on slow or medium speed until the ganache takes on a matt finish.

GLOSSY DARK GLAZE

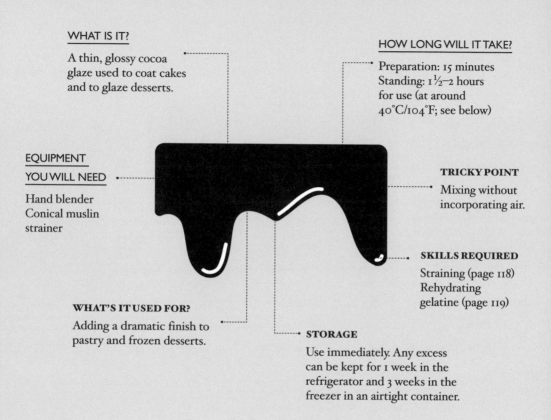

WHAT IS IT?

A thin, glossy cocoa glaze used to coat cakes and to glaze desserts.

HOW LONG WILL IT TAKE?

Preparation: 15 minutes
Standing: 1½–2 hours
for use (at around
40°C/104°F; see below)

**EQUIPMENT
YOU WILL NEED**

Hand blender
Conical muslin
strainer

TRICKY POINT

Mixing without
incorporating air.

SKILLS REQUIRED

Straining (page 118)
Rehydrating
gelatine (page 119)

WHAT'S IT USED FOR?

Adding a dramatic finish to pastry and frozen desserts.

STORAGE

Use immediately. Any excess can be kept for 1 week in the refrigerator and 3 weeks in the freezer in an airtight container.

ADVICE

Glaze should be used at around 40°C (104°F). The cake you are coating must be completely frozen for the glaze to adhere well to the surface. Always have more glaze to hand than required. If the glaze is too hot when poured out, the layer will be too thin. If this happens, put the pastry back in the freezer for 15 minutes and pour the glaze from the baking tray back into the remaining glaze. Take the pastry from the freezer once again and re-glaze. Immediately check how well the glaze is running to avoid unwanted streaks; the glaze on a frozen product sets very quickly.

TIP

Allow as little air as possible to get in while mixing: put the blender head into the glaze without turning it on, move it around gently to let any air bubbles escape, then turn on the blender without moving it for about 30 seconds to 1 minute.

MAKES 750 G (1LB 9 OZ) GLAZE

14 g (7 sheets) gelatine
180 g (6½ oz) water
150 g (5 oz) whipping cream
330 g (11 oz) white caster (superfine) sugar
120 g (4 oz) cocoa (unsweetened chocolate) powder

1. Rehydrate the gelatine (page 119) in cold water. Bring the measured water, cream and sugar to the boil in a saucepan.

2. Remove the pan from the heat and add the gelatine and cocoa powder. Whisk thoroughly. Pour into a measuring glass, mix well (see tip), then pour through the strainer into a bowl. Cover with cling film (plastic wrap), then cool, at room temperature, to 40°C (104°F) before using.

ROCK GLAZE

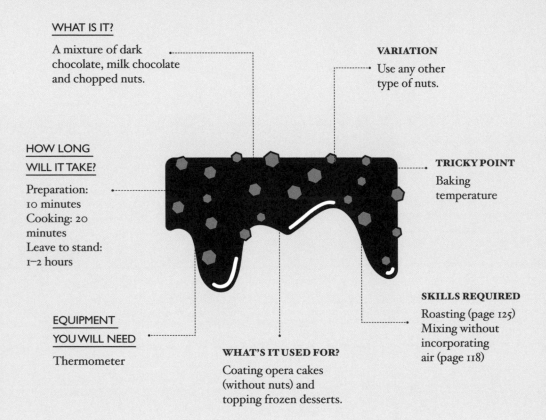

WHAT IS IT?

A mixture of dark chocolate, milk chocolate and chopped nuts.

VARIATION

Use any other type of nuts.

HOW LONG

WILL IT TAKE?

Preparation:
10 minutes
Cooking: 20 minutes
Leave to stand:
1–2 hours

TRICKY POINT

Baking temperature

EQUIPMENT

YOU WILL NEED

Thermometer

SKILLS REQUIRED

Roasting (page 125)
Mixing without incorporating air (page 118)

WHAT'S IT USED FOR?

Coating opera cakes (without nuts) and topping frozen desserts.

TIP

When pouring out the rock glaze, use a spatula to remove the excess from the rack.

ADVICE

Store remaining glaze in a container at room temperature for up to 1 month. To use, melt gently in a double-boiler.

MAKES 300 G (10½ OZ) GLAZE

80 g (3 oz) chopped almonds
130 g (4 oz) milk chocolate
150 g (5 oz) dark chocolate
(66% cocoa)
25 g (1 oz) grapeseed oil

1. Roast the chopped almonds
for 20 minutes in a 160°C
(320°F/gas 4) oven (page
125). Melt the 2 chocolates
together in a double-boiler.

2. Remove the bowl from the
double-boiler, pour in the oil
and gently mix using a spatula,

without incorporating any
air. Let the temperature drop
to around 40°C (104°F). Add
the chopped almonds, mix
well and use immediately.

MILK CHOCOLATE GLAZE

WHAT IS IT?

A versatile chocolate glaze topping.

HOW LONG WILL IT TAKE?

Preparation: 15 minutes

EQUIPMENT YOU WILL NEED

Thermometer

WHAT'S IT USED FOR?

A finish for log cakes, tarts and desserts.

TRICKY POINTS

Mixing without incorporating air

SKILL REQUIRED

Using a double-boiler (page 118)

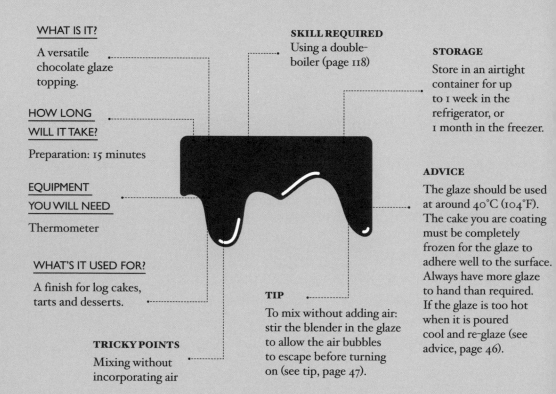

STORAGE

Store in an airtight container for up to 1 week in the refrigerator, or 1 month in the freezer.

ADVICE

The glaze should be used at around 40°C (104°F). The cake you are coating must be completely frozen for the glaze to adhere well to the surface. Always have more glaze to hand than required. If the glaze is too hot when it is poured cool and re-glaze (see advice, page 46).

TIP

To mix without adding air: stir the blender in the glaze to allow the air bubbles to escape before turning on (see tip, page 47).

HOW DOES THE GLAZE STICK TO THE CAKE?

On contact with a frozen cake, the cocoa butter crystallises. The glaze becomes stickier, adheres to the cake, and then hardens as it cools.

MAKES 550 G (1 LB 3 OZ) GLAZE

250 g (9 oz) milk chocolate
90 g (3¼ oz) dark chocolate
225 g whipping cream
40 g (1½ oz) inverted sugar or neutral honey

1. Melt the two chocolates together in a double-boiler (page 118).

2. Heat the cream and inverted sugar or honey together in a saucepan until they begin to boil, then mix using a whisk.

3. Pour the cream and sugar mixture over the melted chocolate, away from the double-boiler, and whisk well. Leave to cool for 1½–2 hours and use when it is 35–40°C (95–104°F).

WHITE CHOCOLATE GLAZE

WHAT IS IT?

A dramatic glaze made from white chocolate.

HOW LONG WILL IT TAKE?

Preparation: 15 minutes
Standing: 2 hours

EQUIPMENT YOU WILL NEED

Hand blender
Conical strainer
Thermometer

VARIATIONS

Add the seeds from 1 vanilla pod (bean) to the milk.
Colour with food colouring.

WHAT'S IT USED FOR?

Coating log cakes, tarts and desserts.

SKILLS REQUIRED

Using a double-boiler (page 118)
Rehydrating gelatine (page 119)
Straining (page 118)

STORAGE

Store in an airtight container for up to 1 week in the refrigerator, 3 weeks in the freezer.

ADVICE

Glaze should be used at around 40°C (104°F), the cake you are coating must be completely frozen and always have more glaze to hand than required. If the glaze is too hot when it is poured, cool and re-glaze (see advice, page 46).

MAKES 500 G (1 LB 2 OZ) GLAZE

6 g (3 sheets) gelatine
300 g (10½ oz) white chocolate
120 g (4 oz) milk
30 g (1 oz) water
50 g (2 oz) glucose syrup

1. Rehydrate the gelatine in cold water (page 119). Melt the white chocolate in a double-boiler (page 118)

2. Heat the milk, water and glucose syrup in a saucepan and bring to the boil. When it boils, take off the heat. Drain the gelatine, add it to the mixture and whisk.

3. Pour this mixture onto the white chocolate and whisk. Remove the bowl from the double-boiler, then blend gently, taking care to add as little air as possible. Leave to stand for a few minutes, then blend again for another 2–3 minutes. Strain (page 118), then cover with cling film (plastic wrap). Allow to cool to room temperature (for use at around 40°C/104°F).

CHAPTER 2

CHOCOLATE RECIPES

SINGLE ORIGIN GANACHE DIPPED CHOCOLATES

Dark chocolate ganache dipped in dark couverture chocolate.

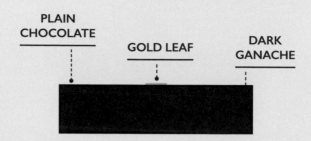

PLAIN
CHOCOLATE

GOLD LEAF

DARK
GANACHE

HOW LONG WILL IT TAKE?

Preparation: 2 hours
Standing: 12 hours (ganache)
Setting: 48 hours

EQUIPMENT REQUIRED

Thermometer
Polyethylene sheets
Piping bag
Chocolate fork

VARIATION

Vary the origins of the chocolate, keeping
the same percentage of cocoa.

TRICKY POINTS

Tempering the couverture chocolate
Coating the chocolates

SKILLS REQUIRED

Tempering chocolate (page 24)
Using a piping bag (page 120)
Coating with a thin layer of
chocolate (chabloning; page 115)
Coating with a dipping fork (page 32)
Decorating (page 36)

ADVICE

If the ganache separates out into
solids and fat, add more milk.
When the chocolates have been dipped,
pour the remaining melted chocolate
onto a baking sheet, leave to harden
and keep in a dry place. Do not temper
it again as it will lose its fluidity.

PLANNING AND PREP

The day before: Ganache
On the day: Dipping

MAKES ABOUT 35 CHOCOLATES

FOR 350 G (12 OZ) GANACHE

190 g (6 ½ oz) dark couverture
chocolate (70% cocoa)
180 g (6 ¼ oz) whipping cream
15 g (½ oz) glucose syrup

10 g (½ oz) inverted sugar or neutral honey
15 g (½ oz) unsalted butter

COATING

800 g (1lb 12 oz) dark couverture
chocolate (70% cocoa)
2 gold leaf fragments

1. Make a dark chocolate ganache: melt the chocolate in a double-boiler (page 118). Meanwhile, put the cream, glucose, inverted sugar/honey and butter in a saucepan and bring to the boil.

2. Strain half of the cream mixture into the chocolate and mix with a whisk to start the emulsion.

3. Strain the rest of the mixture into the chocolate and finish the emulsion by stirring for about 1 minute without incorporating air (page 118). Cover with cling film (plastic wrap) and set aside.

4. Cut a polyethylene sheet into 35 squares measuring 4 × 4 cm (1½ × 1½ in). Place them on another polyethylene sheet. When the ganache is at 35°C (95°F), put

it in a piping bag and pipe out 2 cm (¾ in) diameter domes onto the squares.

5. Place another polyethylene sheet on top, then using a flat tray, press lightly to give the sweets their final shape. Leave to set at 15–17°C (59–63°F) for 12 hours.

6. Temper the coating chocolate (page 24). Coat the tops and bottoms with a fine layer of chocolate (chabloning; page 115).

7. Coat each one by dipping into the melted chocolate using a dipping fork (page 32). Scrape the fork over the rim to remove excess chocolate. Decorate with a gold leaf fragment (pages 37, 125) and immediately place a square of polyethylene sheet on top. Allow to set at room temperature, ideally 15–17°C (59–63°F) for 48 hours.

VANILLA GANACHE DIPPED CHOCOLATES

Dark vanilla flavoured ganache dipped in dark couverture chocolate.

DARK CHOCOLATE — — — DARK VANILLA GANACHE

HOW LONG WILL IT TAKE?

Preparation: 2 hours
Standing: 12 hours (ganache)
Setting: 48 hours

EQUIPMENT YOU WILL NEED

Thermometer
Piping bag
Polyethylene sheet
Dipping fork

VARIATION

Coffee ganache: instead of vanilla,
use 5 g (¼ oz) instant coffee.

TRICKY POINTS

Tempering the couverture chocolate
Coating the chocolates

SKILLS REQUIRED

Tempering chocolate (page 24)
Using a piping bag (page 120)
Coating with a thin layer of
chocolate (chabloning; page 115)
Coating with a dipping fork (page 32)
Decorating (page 36)

PLANNING AND PREP

The day before: Ganache
On the day: Coating

MAKES ABOUT 35 CHOCOLATES

VANILLA GANACHE

200 g (7 oz) dark couverture
chocolate (66% cocoa)
180 g (6¼ oz) whipping cream
1 vanilla pod (bean), split and scraped
15 g (½ oz) glucose syrup
10 g (½ oz) inverted sugar or neutral honey
15 g (½ oz) butter

COATING

800 g (1lb 12 oz) dark couverture
chocolate (66% cocoa)

1. Make the vanilla ganache: melt the
chocolate in a double-boiler (page 118).
Meanwhile, put the cream, split and scraped
vanilla pod, glucose, inverted sugar/honey and
butter in a saucepan and bring to the boil.

2. Strain half of this mixture into the
chocolate and whisk to start the emulsion.

3. Strain the rest of the cream mixture into
the chocolate mixture and mix for about
1 minute without incorporating air (page
118). Cover with cling film (plastic wrap).

4. When the ganache is at 35°C (95°F),
put it in a piping bag and squeeze out
lengths of chocolate. Leave to set at
15–17°C (59–63°F) for 12 hours.

5. Temper the coating chocolate (page
24). Cut the set ganache into 3 cm (1¼ in)
lengths. Coat the undersides with a thin
layer of chocolate (chabloning, page 115).

6. Coat each chocolate using the dipping
fork (page 32). Scrape the fork over the
rim to remove excess chocolate. Allow
to set at room temperature, ideally
15–17°C (59–63°F), for 48 hours.

MILK CHOCOLATE AND CARAMEL MOULDED CHOCOLATES

Moulded dark chocolates filled with caramel and milk chocolate ganache.

DARK CHOCOLATE

DARK GANACHE CARAMEL

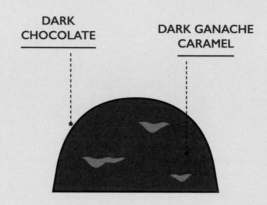

HOW LONG WILL IT TAKE?

Preparation: 2 hours
Standing: 12 hours (after moulding ganache)
Setting: 36 hours (after sealing)

EQUIPMENT YOU WILL NEED

Thermometer
Polycarbonate mould

VARIATION

Instead of cream use passion
fruit or strawberry purée.

TRICKY POINT

Tempering the couverture chocolate

SKILLS REQUIRED

Tempering chocolate (page 24)
Making moulded chocolates (page 34)

ADVICE

Make the caramel in a large pan to prevent
burning when adding the butter and cream.

TIP

When mixing, take care to add as little air as
possible: keep the blender blade on the bottom
of the bowl, stir gently to let the air escape,
then mix for about 1 minute without lifting.

PLANNING AND PREP

The day before: Moulding – ganache
On the day: Sealing
Following day: Unmoulding

MAKES ABOUT 35 CHOCOLATES

GANACHE

200 g (7 oz) whipping cream
100 g (3½ oz) white caster (superfine) sugar
20 g (¾ oz) unsalted butter
2 g (½ teaspoon) sea salt flakes
140 g (4½ oz) dark couverture chocolate (66% cocoa)
170 g (6 oz) milk couverture chocolate

COATING

600 g (1 lb 5 oz) dark couverture chocolate (66% cocoa)

1. Temper two-thirds of the coating chocolate and coat the bottoms of the moulds with it (page 24).

2. Make the ganache: boil the cream, set aside. Make a dry caramel: heat the sugar in a saucepan over a medium–high heat. When it begins to dissolve into caramel, mix with a whisk until it turns a dark colour. Take the pan off the heat and pour in a little cream. Once the cream is completely incorporated, add the butter, then keep adding more cream in small quantities until it is completely blended in. Add the sea salt flakes, then cook for about 30 seconds, stirring all the time.

3. When the mixture boils, pour it into the dark and milk chocolates, then blend without incorporating air (page 118). Cover with cling film (plastic wrap) and set aside.

4. When the ganache is at 27°C (80.6°F), pipe it into the chocolate moulds. Leave to set at 15–17°C (59–62°F) for 12 hours.

5. Temper the remaining coating chocolate (page 24). Seal the chocolates (page 35). Allow to set at room temperature, ideally 15–17°C (59–62°F) for 48 hours.

HONEY GANACHE DIPPED CHOCOLATES

Chestnut honey ganache dipped in milk couverture chocolate.

MILK CHOCOLATE

HONEY GANACHE

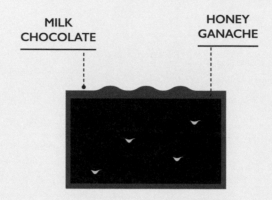

HOW LONG WILL IT TAKE?

Preparation: 2 hours
Standing: 12 hours (ganache)
Setting: 48 hours

EQUIPMENT YOU WILL NEED

15 × 15 cm (6 × 6 in) baking frame
Thermometer
Polyethylene sheet
Dipping fork

VARIATION

Instead of chestnut honey, use mountain or lavender honey.

TRICKY POINTS

Tempering the couverture chocolate
Coating the chocolates

SKILLS REQUIRED

Tempering chocolate (page 24)
Coating with a thin layer of chocolate (chabloning; page 115)
Coating with a dipping fork (page 32)
Decorating (page 36)

PLANNING AND PREP

The day before: Ganache
On the day: Dipping

MAKES ABOUT 35 CHOCOLATES

HONEY GANACHE

200 g (7 oz) milk couverture chocolate
200 g (7 oz) whipping cream
75 g (2½ oz) cocoa butter
75 g (2½ oz) chestnut honey

COATING

800 g (1lb 12 oz) milk couverture chocolate

1. Prepare 200 g (7 oz) of the chocolate coating and the baking frame (page 32). Make the honey ganache: melt the chocolate in a double-boiler (page 118). Bring the cream and cocoa butter to the boil and set aside.

2. Meanwhile, heat the honey to 130°C (266°F). Remove from the heat and gradually mix in the cream/cocoa butter mixture.

3. Strain half of this mixture into the chocolate and mix with a whisk to

start the emulsion. Strain the rest into the chocolate and finish the emulsion by mixing for about 1 minute without incorporating air (page 118). Cover with cling film (plastic wrap) and set aside.

4. When the ganache is at 32°C (89.6°F), pour it into the baking frame, smooth the top, then let it set (page 25) for 10–12 hours at 15–17°C (59–62°F).

5. Temper the rest of the coating couverture. Remove the ganache from the frame by running the blade of a knife along the edges (page 115). Coat the upper surface of the ganache with a thin layer of chocolate (page 115). Before the thin layer cools completely, cut out 1½ × 3 cm (½ in × 1¼ in) chocolates.

6. Coat each one by dipping it into the tempered chocolate using a dipping fork (page 32). Scrape the fork on the rim to remove excess chocolate, then decorate (page 36). Leave to set at room temperature, ideally 15–17°C (59–62°F) for 48 hours.

VERBENA GANACHE DIPPED CHOCOLATES

Ganache flavoured with verbena, made with eggs and coated with dark chocolate.

DARK CHOCOLATE   **VERBENA GANACHE**

HOW LONG WILL IT TAKE?

Preparation: 2 hours
Standing: 12 hours (ganache)
Setting: 48 hours

EQUIPMENT YOU WILL NEED

Thermometer
Polyethylene sheet
Piping bag
Dipping fork

VARIATION

Instead of verbena use the same amount
of mint or a sprig of rosemary.

TRICKY POINTS

Tempering the couverture chocolate

Coating the chocolates

SKILLS REQUIRED

Tempering chocolate (page 24)
Using a piping bag (page 120)
Coating with a thin layer of
chocolate (chabloning; page 115)
Coating with a dipping fork (page 32)
Decorating (page 36)

ADVICE

For the best herbal flavour, let the verbena
soak in the cream overnight in the refrigerator.

PLANNING AND PREP

The day before: Ganache
On the day: Dipping
Following day: Ready to serve
Keep for: 1 week maximum

VERBENA GANACHE

140 g (4 ½ oz) whipping cream
½ bunch of verbena
25 g (1 oz) inverted sugar or neutral honey
25 g (1 oz) egg yolks (2 yolks)
200 g (7 oz) dark couverture
chocolate (66% cocoa)

COATING

800 g (1lb 12 oz) dark couverture
chocolate (66% cocoa)

1. Make the verbena ganache: heat the cream with the verbena in a saucepan, bring to the boil then take off the heat, cover with cling film (plastic wrap) and leave to infuse for 30 minutes.

2. Strain the mixture into another saucepan and top up with cream to return to 140 g

(4 ½ oz). Add the inverted sugar/honey and egg yolks and mix. Heat the mixture to 85°C (185°F), stirring with a whisk. Add the chocolate, mix, then blend without incorporating air (page 118). Cover with cling film (plastic wrap) and set aside.

3. Cover a baking tray with a polyethylene sheet. When the ganache is at 27°C (80.6°F), put it in a piping bag and pipe out 1.5 cm (½ in) diameter rolls the entire length of the tray. Leave to set for 10–12 hours at 15–17°C (59–62°F).

4. Cut the rolls into short 2.5 cm (1 in) lengths. Temper the coating chocolate (page 24). Coat the underside of the ganache with a fine layer of chocolate (page 115).

5. Dip each chocolate (page 32) into the coating chocolate, scrape the fork on the rim to remove excess and decorate using a cone (page 36). Allow to set at room temperature, ideally 15–17°C (59–62°F) for 48 hours.

MINT CHOCOLATE MOULDED CHOCOLATES

*Moulded chocolates made of white chocolate with a green decoration
and filled with mint-flavoured milk chocolate ganache.*

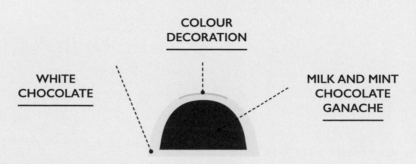

COLOUR
DECORATION

WHITE
CHOCOLATE

MILK AND MINT
CHOCOLATE
GANACHE

HOW LONG WILL IT TAKE?

Preparation: 2 hours
Standing: 12 hours (after moulding ganache)
Setting: 48 hours (after sealing)

EQUIPMENT YOU WILL NEED

Thermometer
Polycarbonate mould

VARIATION

Instead of mint, use another flavouring.

TRICKY POINT

Tempering the couverture chocolate

SKILLS REQUIRED

Tempering chocolate (page 24)
Making moulded chocolates (page 34)

ADVICE

It is important to use a fat-soluble
colouring agent. Mix it in two stages,
waiting 5 minutes between each
addition to ensure even colouring.
Leave the mint to soak in the cream
overnight in the refrigerator.

TIP

Straining the cream results in a slight
loss of quantity. Weigh the strained
cream and top up if necessary.

PLANNING AND PREP

The day before: Moulding – ganache
On the day: Sealing
After 2 days: Unmoulding

MAKES ABOUT 50 CHOCOLATES

MINT GANACHE

115 g (4 oz) whipping cream
¼ bunch of mint
170 g (6 oz) milk couverture chocolate
25 g (1 oz) unsalted butter

COLOUR DECORATION

1 g cocoa butter
70 g (2½ oz) white couverture chocolate
1 drop of fat-soluble green colouring

COATING

600 g (1 1lb 5 oz) white couverture chocolate

1. Make the decoration mixture: melt the cocoa butter and white couverture chocolate in a double-boiler at 40°C (104°F). Add the colouring and mix in two stages, waiting 5 minutes between each, then temper (page 24).

2. Using a dry brush, paint the bottom of the imprints of the mould with a broad stroke of green couverture chocolate. Temper two-thirds of the coating white chocolate and put it into the mould (page 36).

3. Make the mint ganache: heat the cream and mint in a saucepan and, when it boils, take off the heat, cover and leave to infuse for 30 minutes. Strain into another saucepan. Top up the cream to 115 g (4 oz), boil briefly, then pour over the milk couverture. Blend, then cover with cling film (plastic wrap).

4. When the ganache is at 35°C (95°F), add the softened butter, then mix. When at 32°C (89.6°F), pipe out into the moulds. Leave to set for 10–12 hours.

5. Temper the remaining white coating couverture (page 24). Seal the chocolates (page 35) and leave to set (page 29) for 48 hours at room temperature, ideally 15–17°C (59–62°F).

RASPBERRY GANACHE DIPPED CHOCOLATES

Raspberry milk and dark couverture ganache dipped in dark chocolate.

DARK CHOCOLATE

RASPBERRY GANACHE

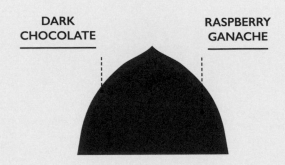

HOW LONG WILL IT TAKE?

Preparation: 2 hours
Standing: 12 hours (ganache)
Setting: 48 hours

EQUIPMENT YOU WILL NEED

Thermometer
Polyethylene sheet
Piping bag
Dipping fork

VARIATION

Instead of raspberry, use passion fruit purée.

TRICKY POINTS

Tempering the couverture chocolate
Coating the chocolates

SKILLS REQUIRED

Tempering chocolate (page 24)
Using a piping bag (page 120)
Coating with a thin layer of
chocolate (chabloning; page 115)
Coating with a dipping fork (page 32)
Decorating (page 36)

ADVICE

To give a stronger raspberry taste, replace
the raspberry cream with raspberry brandy.
Decorate with dehydrated raspberry chips.

PLANNING AND PREP

The day before: Ganache
On the day: Dipping

MAKES ABOUT 35 CHOCOLATES

RASPBERRY GANACHE

150 g (5 oz) dark couverture
chocolate (66% cocoa)
165 g (5½ oz) milk couverture chocolate
100 g (3½ oz) raspberry purée
20 g (¾ oz) white caster (superfine) sugar
2 g NH pectin (thermally reversible
pectin, from specialist suppliers)
75 g (2½ oz) whipping cream
40 g (1½ oz) unsalted butter
10 g (½ oz) inverted sugar or neutral honey
20 g (¾ oz) raspberry cream

COATING

800 g (1lb 12 oz) dark couverture (66% cocoa)

1. To make the raspberry ganache: melt the
two types of chocolate in a double-boiler
(page 118). Boil the raspberry purée. Mix the
sugar and pectin and add to the raspberry
purée, then cook for 30 seconds and set aside.

2. Put the cream, butter and inverted
sugar/honey in a saucepan and bring to the
boil. Pour the hot mixture into the melted
chocolate, then add the sweet raspberry purée
and the raspberry cream. Whisk to start
the emulsion, then mix for about 1 minute
without incorporating air (page 118). Cover
with cling film (plastic wrap) and set aside.

3. Place a polyethylene sheet on a baking tray.
When the ganache is at 35°C (95°F), pipe out
large drops (page 120) onto the polyethylene
sheet. Leave to set for 10–12 hours at room
temperature, ideally 15–17°C (59–62°F).

4. Temper the coating couverture (page 24).
Coat the underside of the ganache with a
thin layer of chocolate (page 115). Coat by
dipping each chocolate into the tempered
chocolate with a fork (page 32). Scrape
the fork over the rim to remove excess
chocolate. Allow to set at room temperature,
ideally 15–17°C (59–62°F) for 48 hours.

GRAND MARNIER MOULDED CHOCOLATES

Milk chocolate moulded sweets filled with Grand Marnier ganache.

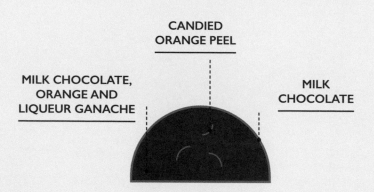

CANDIED ORANGE PEEL

MILK CHOCOLATE, ORANGE AND LIQUEUR GANACHE

MILK CHOCOLATE

HOW LONG WILL IT TAKE?

Preparation: 2 hours
Standing: 12 hours (after moulding ganache)
Setting: 48 hours (after sealing)

EQUIPMENT YOU WILL NEED

Thermometer
Polycarbonate mould
Polyethylene sheet

VARIATION

Replace the Grand Marnier with another
spirit: whisky, rum or calvados.

TRICKY POINT

Tempering the couverture chocolate

SKILLS REQUIRED

Tempering chocolate (page 24)
Making moulded chocolates (page 34)

TIP

When mixing, take care to incorporate as little
air as possible: push the stem of the mixer
down to the bottom of the bowl and stir gently
to allow air to escape from the blades. Mix
for about 1 minute without lifting the mixer.

PLANNING AND PREP

The day before: Moulding – ganache
On the day: Sealing
Two days later: Unmoulding

GANACHE

100 g (3½ oz) whipping cream
200 g (7 oz) milk couverture chocolate
30 g (1 oz) candied orange peel
35 g (1 oz) Grand Marnier

COATING

600 g (1 lb 5 oz) milk chocolate couverture

1. Temper the coating chocolate
and coat the moulds (page 24).

2. Make the ganache: boil the cream and set
aside. Melt the chocolate in a double-boiler
(page 118). Mix the chocolate with the cream
and blend without incorporating air (page
118). Cover with cling film (plastic wrap).

3. Finely chop the orange peel with a
knife. When the cream-chocolate mixture
is at 25°C (77°F), add the Grand Marnier.

4. Pipe out into the chocolate-coated
moulds, then scatter over the orange
peel. Leave to set for 10–12 hours at room
temperature, ideally 15–17°C (59–62°F).

5. Temper the remaining coating couverture
and seal the chocolates (page 35). Allow to
set for 48 hours at room temperature.

SESAME & HAZELNUT DIPPED CHOCOLATES

Hazelnut praline and sesame paste interior dipped in milk chocolate couverture.

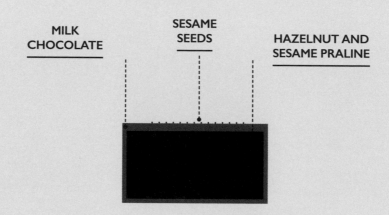

MILK CHOCOLATE

SESAME SEEDS

HAZELNUT AND SESAME PRALINE

HOW LONG WILL IT TAKE?

Preparation: 3 hours
Standing: 12 hours (hazelnut-sesame interior)
Setting: 48 hours

EQUIPMENT YOU WILL NEED

Blender
15 × 15 cm (6 × 6 in) baking frame
Thermometer
Polyethylene sheet
Dipping fork

TRICKY POINTS

Tempering the couverture chocolate

Coating the chocolates

SKILLS REQUIRED

Making praline (page 40)
Tempering chocolate (page 24)
Coating with a thin layer of
chocolate (chabloning; page 115)
Coating with a dipping fork (page 32)
Decorating (page 36)

PLANNING AND PREP

2 days before: Praline – sesame paste
The day before: Hazelnut-sesame interior
On the day: Dipping

MAKES ABOUT 35 CHOCOLATES

HAZELNUT PRALINE

100 g (3½ oz) shelled hazelnuts
100 g (3½ oz) white caster (superfine) sugar
35 g (1 oz) water

SESAME PASTE

200 g black sesame seeds

HAZELNUT – SESAME GIANDUJA

50 g (2 oz) milk couverture chocolate
150 g (5 oz) hazelnut praline (from left)
190 g (6½ oz) sesame paste (from left)
50 g (2 oz) cocoa butter

COATING

800 g (1lb 12 oz) milk couverture chocolate

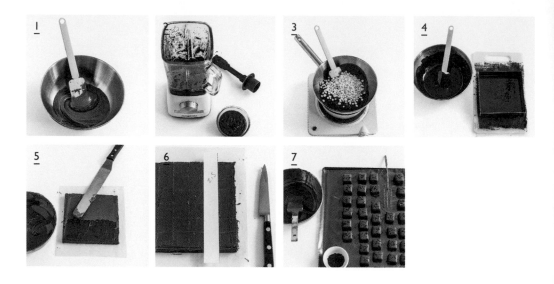

1. Make the hazelnut praline (page 40).

2. Make the sesame paste: roast the sesame seeds in a pan over a low heat for 5–10 minutes, stirring regularly. Transfer to a baking tray and leave to cool. Process in a blender, scraping down the sides of the bowl 2 or 3 times using a spatula; a thin layer of oil will appear on the surface.

3. Temper 200 g (7 oz) of the coating chocolate and prepare the baking frame (page 24). To make the hazelnut-sesame gianduja: melt the chocolate in a double-boiler (page 118). Mix together the sesame paste and hazelnut praline, then add the cocoa butter and chocolate.

4. When the filling is at 30°C (86°F),

pour it into the frame, smooth out and leave to set for 10–12 hours at room temperature, ideally 15–17°C (59–62°F).

5. Temper the rest of the coating chocolate. Remove the hazelnut-sesame gianduja from the frame by running the blade of a knife along the edges (page 115). Coat the top with a fine layer of chocolate (page 115).

6. Before the fine chocolate topping layer has cooled completely, cut out 2.5 × 2.5 cm (1 × 1 in) chocolates.

7. Coat the chocolates using a dipping fork (page 32) and immediately sprinkle with sesame seeds (page 36). Allow to set at room temperature, ideally 15–17°C (59–62°F) for 48 hours.

PRALINE FEUILLETINE CHOCOLATES

A crispy praline and feuilletine centre coated with dark chocolate.

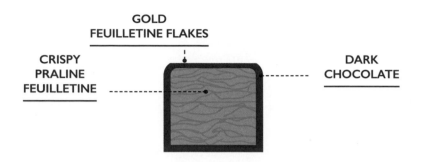

GOLD FEUILLETINE FLAKES

CRISPY PRALINE FEUILLETINE

DARK CHOCOLATE

HOW LONG WILL IT TAKE?

Preparation: 2 hours
Standing: 12 hours (ganache)
Setting: 48 hours

EQUIPMENT YOU WILL NEED

Thermometer
15 × 15 cm (6 × 6 in) baking frame
Stand mixer with flat beater attachment
Polyethylene sheet
Dipping fork

TRICKY POINTS

Tempering the couverture chocolate
Coating the chocolates

SKILLS REQUIRED

Tempering chocolate (page 24)
Making praline (page 40)
Coating with a thin layer of
chocolate (chabloning; page 115)
Coating with a dipping fork (page 32)

PLANNING AND PREP

Previous day: Ganache
On the day: Dipping

MAKES ABOUT 35 CHOCOLATES

PRALINE

75 g (2½ oz) shelled almonds
75 g (2½ oz) shelled hazelnuts
150 g (5 oz) white caster (superfine) sugar
60 g (2 oz) water

CRISPY PRALINE FEUILLETINE

45 g (1¾ oz) dark couverture
chocolate (66% cocoa)
20 g (¾ oz) cocoa butter
250 g (9 oz) praline (from above)
125 g (4 oz) feuilletine flakes (crushed
crispy crêpes; from specialist suppliers)

COATING AND DECORATION

800 g (1lb 12 oz) dark couverture
chocolate (66% cocoa)
10 g (½ oz) feuilletine flakes
1 pinch of gold powder

1. Temper the coating chocolate and
prepare the baking frame (page 24).
Make the praline (page 40). To make
the crispy praline feuilletine: melt the
chocolate and cocoa butter in a double-
boiler to 45°C (113°F) (page 118), then
reduce the temperature to 29°C (84°F).

2. Mix the praline in the bowl of the stand
mixer fitted with the flat beater, pouring
in the chocolate-cocoa butter preparation
until well blended. The temperature
should drop to around 24–25°C (75–77°F).

3. Add the feuilletine and finish by mixing
gently using a spatula to prevent breaking
the feuilletine as much as possible.

4. Pour the feuilletine into the baking frame
1 cm (½ in) deep, cover with the polyethylene
sheet, then leave to set for 10–12 hours at
room temperature, ideally 15–17°C (59–62°F).

5. Temper the rest of the coating chocolate.
Prepare the decoration: crush the feuilletine
by hand in a bowl and add the gold powder.
Remove the feuilletine from the frame by
running the blade of a knife along the edges
(page 115). Coat the top with a thin layer of
chocolate (chabloning; page 115), leave to set
for a few minutes, then turn over. Before
the chocolate coating has cooled completely,
cut out 3 × 1.5 cm (1¼ × ½ in) chocolates.

6. Dip the chocolates (page 32): scrape
the fork on the rim to remove excess
chocolate and decorate immediately with
the feuilletine mixed with gold (page 36).

7. Allow to set at room temperature,
ideally 15–17°C (59–62°F), for 48 hours.

GIANDUJA MOULDED CHOCOLATES

Milk chocolate moulded chocolates filled with milk chocolate and gianduja ganache.

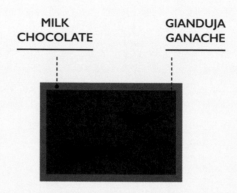

MILK
CHOCOLATE

GIANDUJA
GANACHE

HOW LONG WILL IT TAKE?

Preparation: 2 hours
Standing: 12 hours (after moulding ganache)
Setting: 48 hours (after sealing)

EQUIPMENT YOU WILL NEED

Polycarbonate mould
Thermometer
Polyethylene sheet

TRICKY POINT

Tempering the couverture chocolate

SKILL REQUIRED

Tempering chocolate (page 24)
Making moulded chocolates (page 34)

Making gianduja (page 40)

ADVICE

Excess gianduja will keep in a sealed
container for up to 2 weeks at room
temperature for use in another recipe.

TIP

When mixing, incorporate as little air as
possible: keep the stem of the blender at the
bottom of the bowl, stir to allow air to escape,
and mix for about 1 minute without lifting.

PLANNING AND PREP

The day before: Moulding – ganache
On the day: Sealing
2 days later: Unmoulding

MAKES ABOUT 20

GIANDUJA

25 g (1 oz) shelled almonds
25 g (1 oz) shelled hazelnuts
20 g (¾ oz) water
50 g (2 oz) white caster
(superfine) sugar
60 g (2 oz) dark chocolate
(66% cocoa)

GIANDUJA GANACHE

150 g (5 oz) milk
couverture chocolate
40 g (½ oz) gianduja
(from above)
65 g (2½ oz) whipping cream
25 g (1 oz) inverted sugar

or neutral honey
30 g (1 oz) unsalted butter

COATING

600 g (1 1lb 5 oz) milk
couverture chocolate

1. Temper two-thirds of the
coating chocolate and coat
the moulds (page 24). Make
the gianduja (page 40).

2. To make the ganache:
melt the chocolate in a
double-boiler (page 118)
and add the gianduja
away from the heat.

3. Put the cream and
inverted sugar/honey

in a saucepan and
bring to the boil.

4. Pour over the ganache
mixture. Mix together. Add
the butter and blend. Cover
with cling film (plastic
wrap) and set aside.

5. When the ganache is at
27°C (80.6°F), pipe it out
into the chocolate moulds,
then leave to set for 10–12
hours at room temperature,
ideally 15–17°C (59–62°F).

6. Temper the remaining
coating chocolate. Seal the
chocolates (page 35) and
leave to set for 48 hours
at room temperature.

GIANDUJA ROCK CHOCOLATES

Round gianduja rock chocolates covered with dark chocolate and chopped almonds.

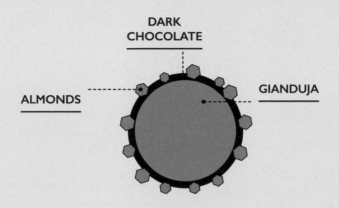

DARK CHOCOLATE

ALMONDS

GIANDUJA

HOW LONG WILL IT TAKE?

Preparation: 2 hours
Cooking: 20 minutes
Standing: 12 hours (ganache)
Setting: 48 hours

EQUIPMENT YOU WILL NEED

Thermometer
Piping bag
Kitchen gloves
Polyethylene sheet

VARIATIONS

Replace 10 g (½ oz) of the chopped
almonds with 10 g (½ oz) finely
chopped candied oranges.
Instead of dark chocolate, use milk chocolate;
instead of almonds, use more hazelnuts.

TRICKY POINTS

Tempering the couverture chocolate
Coating the chocolates

SKILLS REQUIRED

Roasting (page 125)
Tempering chocolate (page 24)
Using a piping bag (page 120)
Coating with a dipping fork (page 32)

TIP

If you prefer the almonds to be visible,
roll the rocks in the chopped almonds
after dipping rather than mixing
them into the coating chocolate.

PLANNING AND PREP

The day before: Praline – gianduja
On the day: Coating – setting
2 days later: Serve

MAKES ABOUT 30

GIANDUJA

50 g (2 oz) shelled almonds
50 g (2 oz) shelled hazelnuts
35 g (1 oz) water
100 g (3½ oz) white
caster (superfine) sugar
120 g (4 oz) dark couverture
chocolate (66% cocoa)

SHAPING

40 g (1½ oz) icing
(confectioner's) sugar

COATING

500 g (1 lb 2 oz) dark
couverture chocolate
(66% cocoa)

40 g (1½ oz) chopped
almonds

1. Make the gianduja (page 40). When the gianduja is at about 35°C (95°F), pipe out walnut-size domes. Leave to set for 12 hours at room temperature.

2. Roast (page 125) the chopped almonds for 20 minutes at 160°C (320°F/ gas 4), then leave to cool. Wearing kitchen gloves, put a thin layer of icing sugar in the palm of your hand to prevent the gianduja from sticking. Roll the domes into balls, working quickly so that the gianduja does not melt.

3. Temper the coating chocolate (page 24). Wearing kitchen gloves, put some of the chocolate in the palm of your hand. Roll onto the balls and put them on a baking sheet lined with baking parchment.

4. Stir the chopped almonds into the rest of the coating chocolate and, wearing kitchen gloves, put some of the almond-couverture chocolate in the palm of your hand. Once again, roll onto the balls. Put each rock on the polyethylene sheet. Allow to set at room temperature, ideally 15–17°C (59–62°F) for 48 hours.

VANILLA & COCONUT ROCK CHOCOLATES

Round chocolates made of white vanilla ganache, filled with a hazelnut and coated with white couverture chocolate and grated coconut.

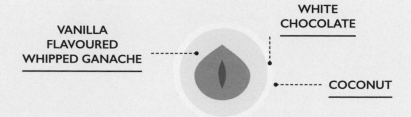

VANILLA FLAVOURED WHIPPED GANACHE

WHITE CHOCOLATE

COCONUT

HOW LONG WILL IT TAKE?

Preparation: 90 minutes
Cooking: 20 minutes
Freezing: 6 hours
Standing: 6–24 hours

EQUIPMENT YOU WILL NEED

Thermometer
Stand mixer with flat beater attachment
Piping bag with 8 mm (⅓ in) plain nozzle
Spherical mould
Kitchen gloves
Dipping fork

VARIATION

Replace the vanilla with 15 g
(½ oz) pistachio paste.

TRICKY POINT

Whipping up ganache

SKILLS REQUIRED

Tempering chocolate using the
Mycryo method (page 30)
Roasting (page 125)
Using a piping bag (120)
Making moulded chocolates (page 34)

TIP

Use semi-spherical moulds: fill, press a
hazelnut into each, then freeze for 4 hours.
Unmould and return to the freezer. Re-fill
the mould, put the frozen halves on top to
complete the spheres, rolling so they stick
together, then freeze for 4–24 hours. Coat.

PLANNING AND PREP

2 days before: Roasting – ganache
The day before: Moulding
On the day: Coating

MAKES ABOUT 70

30 g whole shelled hazelnuts

VANILLA GANACHE

2 g (1 sheet) sheet gelatine
250 g (9 oz) whipping cream
2 vanilla pods (beans), split and scraped
150 g (5 oz) white chocolate

COATING

80 g (3 oz) desiccated (dried
shredded) coconut
3 g (⅒ oz) cocoa butter
300 g (10½ oz) white chocolate

1. Roast the hazelnuts (page 125) for about
20 minutes at 170°C (340°F/gas 3). Leave
to cool, then set aside in a dry place.

2. Make the vanilla ganache (page 44),
adding the split and scraped vanilla
beans (pods) to the cream. Strain
before pouring over the chocolate.

3. After leaving to stand, put the cold
ganache in the bowl of the stand mixer fitted
with the flat beater mix at low–medium
power until it thickens. Transfer to a piping
bag fitted with an 8 mm (⅓ in) plain nozzle.

4. Place the mould on a baking tray. Fill the
lower half of the spheres almost to the top,
add a roasted hazelnut to each, pressing it
in lightly, and cover with the top half of the
mould. Fill up the spheres through the holes.
Tap the tray lightly on the work surface
to remove air bubbles. Re-fill if necessary.
Put in the freezer for at least 6 hours.

5. Cover a sheet of baking parchment with
the coconut. Temper the white couverture
using the Mycryo method (page 30).

6. Unmould the spheres. Wearing
kitchen gloves, put some couverture
chocolate in the palm of your hand. Roll
the spheres, then using a dipping fork,
dip them in the chocolate and remove.
Shake lightly to remove the excess, then
roll them immediately in the coconut.

CARAMEL AND CHOCOLATE FUDGE

Soft caramel fudge with chocolate and vanilla.

CARAMEL CHOCOLATE
VANILLA FUDGE

Preparation: 1 hour
Standing: 12 hours

EQUIPMENT YOU WILL NEED

Silicone sheet
15 × 15 cm (6 × 6 in) baking frame
Thermometer

VARIATION

Add candied ginger cubes before
pouring into the frame.

TRICKY POINTS

Cooking the caramel
Pouring the thick mix

SKILLS REQUIRED

Incorporating liquid into a
caramel (page 61, step 2)

ADVICE

When incorporating the cream into the
syrup, make sure that the temperature
does not fall below 110°C (230°F) so that
the mixture is smooth. To make a hard
caramel, cook the mixture at 121°C (250°F).
After cutting the sweets, wrap well
in cling film (plastic wrap) to prevent
any moisture from getting in.

PLANNING AND PREP

The day before: Caramel
On the day: Cutting and wrapping

MAKES ABOUT 35 CHOCOLATES

50 g (2 oz) water
215 g (7 ½ oz) white caster (superfine) sugar
20 g (¾ oz) glucose syrup
135 g (4 ½ oz) whipping cream
1 vanilla pod (bean), split and scraped
90 g (3 ¼ oz) unsalted butter
2 g (½ teaspoon) salt
70 g (2 ½ oz) pure cocoa paste

1. Put the silicone sheet on a baking tray and place the baking frame on it. Put the water then the sugar in a saucepan and bring to the boil, stirring. Remove the pan from the heat, then brush down the sides of the pan using a wet brush. Add the glucose syrup and cook again, to 145°C (293°F) without stirring.

2. Meanwhile, heat the cream with the scraped vanilla pod. When the cream boils, decrease the heat to lowest, remove the vanilla bean and add the butter and salt.

3. Add the cream to the caramel in several stages, stirring (page 61).

4. Stir in the cocoa paste, increase the heat and cook to 118°C (244°F). Pour immediately into the frame, allow to cool and then cover with cling film (plastic wrap) to protect from moisture. Leave to stand for 12 hours.

5. Remove from the frame by running the blade of a knife along the edges (page 115). Cut out 2.5 × 2.5 cm (1 × 1 in) square chocolates.

TRUFFLES

Dark chocolate-coated ganache rolled in cocoa (unsweetened chocolate) powder.

COCOA

**DARK
CHOCOLATE**

**DARK CHOCOLATE
GANACHE**

HOW LONG WILL IT TAKE?

Preparation: 2 hours
Standing: 12 hours (ganache)
Setting: 48 hours

EQUIPMENT YOU WILL NEED

Thermometer
Piping bag with a 10 mm (½ in) nozzle
Kitchen gloves
Dipping fork

VARIATIONS

Flavour the ganache with any spice you
like, such as Sichuan or Espelette pepper

TRICKY POINTS

Tempering the couverture chocolate
Coating the chocolates

SKILLS REQUIRED

Tempering chocolate (page 24)
Using a piping bag (page 120)
Coating with a dipping fork (page 32)

PLANNING AND PREP

The day before: Ganache
On the day: Coating – setting
2 days later: Ready to enjoy

MAKES ABOUT 35 CHOCOLATES

FOR 350 G (12 OZ) GANACHE

190 g (6 ½ oz) dark couverture
chocolate (66% cocoa)
130 g (4 oz) whipping cream
30 g (1 oz) milk
15 g (½ oz) unsalted butter
15 g (½ oz) glucose syrup
10 g (½ oz) inverted sugar or neutral honey

SHAPING

40 g (1 ½ oz) icing (confectioner's) sugar

COATING

600 g (1 1lb 5 oz) dark couverture
chocolate (66% cocoa)
60 g (2 oz) cocoa (unsweetened
chocolate) powder

1. To make the dark ganache: melt the
chocolate in a double-boiler (page 118).
Meanwhile, put the cream, milk, butter,
glucose syrup and inverted sugar/honey
in a saucepan and bring to the boil.

2. Strain half of this mixture into the
chocolate and whisk to start the emulsion.
Strain the rest into the chocolate and
finish the emulsion by stirring for about
1 minute without letting any air in. Cover
with cling film (plastic wrap) and set aside.

3. When the ganache is at 35°C (95°F),
put it in a piping bag with a 10 mm
(½ in) nozzle, press out 2 cm (¾ in)
dome shapes (page 120) and leave to set
for 12 hours at room temperature.

4. Wearing kitchen gloves, put a thin
layer of icing sugar on your hand to
prevent the ganache from sticking.
Roll the domes into balls.

5. Temper the coating couverture (page 25).
Wearing kitchen gloves, put some of the
chocolate in the palm of your hand. Roll
the balls in it, then dip into the couverture
with a dipping fork (page 32). Roll in cocoa
powder, then roll in a sieve to remove excess
cocoa. Leave to set at room temperature,
ideally 15–17°C (59–62°F), for 48 hours.

CHOCOLATE EGG

Chocolate made in an egg-shaped mould and filled with chocolate pieces.

**DARK
CHOCOLATE**

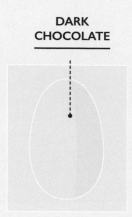

HOW LONG WILL IT TAKE?

Preparation: 2 hours
Setting: 48 hours

EQUIPMENT YOU WILL NEED

Polycarbonate egg moulds (20 cm/8 in)
Pastry ring
Polyethylene sheet
Transparent acetate strip
Piping bag

VARIATION

Use milk or white couverture. If you
use both, temper them separately.

SKILLS REQUIRED

Tempering chocolate (page 24)
Decorating (page 36)

ADVICE

Do not hold the mould directly in your
hands to prevent it from warming. Use
kitchen gloves to prevent fingermarks.

PLANNING AND PREP

2 days before: Moulding
On the day: Decoration – sealing

MAKES A 20 CM (8 IN) EGG

1 kg (2 lb 4 oz) chocolate
(minimum 60% cocoa)
150 g (5 oz) chocolate pieces (of your choice)

1. Clean the mould thoroughly with a clean cloth to remove any dust or fingermarks. Place the pastry ring on a polyethylene sheet and secure with some transparent acetate strip.

2. Temper 900 g (2 lb) of the couverture chocolate (page 24). Using a brush, apply a thin layer of couverture to each half of the mould to start making the two egg halves. Allow to set for a few minutes, then scrape off any excess (page 113). Fill the pastry ring with 1 cm (½ in) of couverture chocolate to make the stand for the egg.

3. Fill a half-egg mould with couverture chocolate, tap the mould to allow air bubbles to escape, turn over and run off most of the chocolate, tapping continuously, then place on pastry rings to finish emptying the excess chocolate. Do the same with the second half-egg.

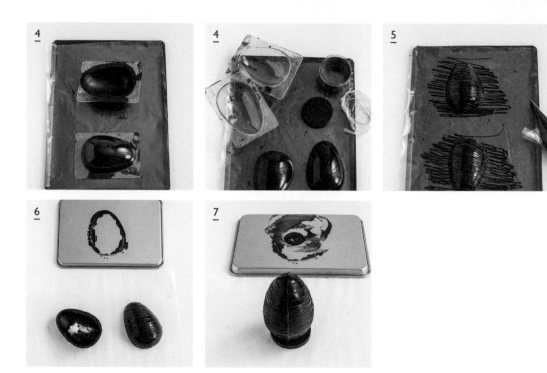

4. After a few minutes, scrape off the rough edges, pour another layer of chocolate into each egg half and place directly on a baking sheet to make a flat surface for sealing. Allow to set at room temperature, ideally 15–17°C (59–62°F) for 48 hours.

5. To unmould the egg halves, slide them to one side, ensuring you touch only the inside of the chocolate. Remove the ring and the acetate tape. Temper the remaining couverture chocolate (page 24). Using a piping bag (page 120), decorate the egg halves with thin lines of chocolate (page 36).

6. Heat a baking tray on a double-boiler (page 118). Wearing kitchen gloves, place an egg half on the warm tray for a few seconds to slightly melt the flat surface, then remove and fill with chocolate pieces. Place the second egg half on the warm baking tray, then immediately put them together to form and seal the egg.

7. Wait a few minutes for the egg to seal properly, then warm the base of the egg and put it on the stand.

CHOCOLATE BOX

Chocolate moulded in the shape of a cylindrical box.

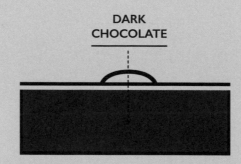

DARK CHOCOLATE

HOW LONG WILL IT TAKE?

Preparation: 2 hours
Standing: 48 hours (setting)

EQUIPMENT YOU WILL NEED

24 cm (9 ½ in) pastry ring
22 cm (8 ½ in) pastry ring
8 cm (3 in) pastry ring
6 cm (2 ½ in) pastry ring
Transparent acetate strip
Thermometer
Triangular spatula
Wire brush

TRICKY POINT

Brushing
Tempering the couverture chocolate

SKILLS REQUIRED

Tempering chocolate (page 24)

PLANNING AND PREP

2 days before: Moulding
On the day: Brushing – finishing

ADVICE

Be sure to brush on several coats of chocolate to make the base of the box: the cling film (plastic wrap) used to support the base is much less rigid than the metal ring around the circumference. If you plan to fill the finished box with chocolates, the base needs to be quite strong.
Take care not to damage the chocolate box when using the wire brush.
Remove the chocolate dust using a dry brush.

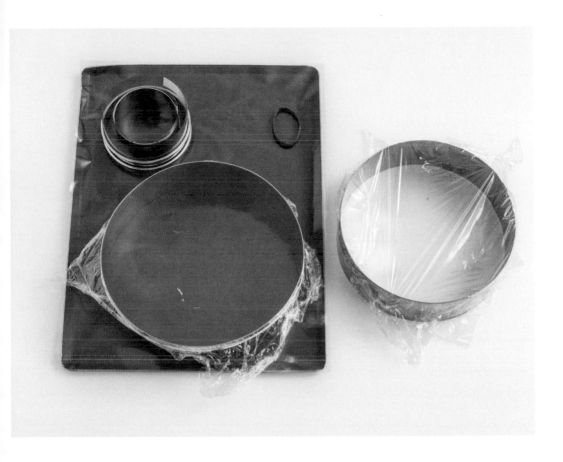

MAKES A 22 CM (8½ IN) BOX

1.2 kg (2 lb 4 oz) dark couverture chocolate (minimum 60% cocoa)

PREPARE THE EQUIPMENT

For the box and the lid: cover the bottom of the two larger rings with cling film, holding it in place on the sides with an elastic (rubber) band. For the handle: cover the base of the 8 cm (3 in) pastry ring with cling film and line the inside of the rim with a strip of transparent acetate strip. Line the outer rim of the 6 cm (2½ in) ring with a strip of transparent acetate strip and place it inside the 8 cm (3 in) ring.

1. Temper the couverture chocolate (page 24). To make the lid: cover the bottom of the lined 24 cm (9½ in) ring with a layer of chocolate 5 mm (¼ in) thick. To make the handle: fill the outer ring formed by the two small lined rings of different diameters to a depth of 1 cm (½ in).

2. For the box: brush a thin layer of chocolate onto the rim and the base of the 22 cm (8½ in) ring. Leave to set for a few minutes, then scrape the sides clean (page 113). Repeat this operation three or four times until a strong base has been formed.

3. For the sides: fill the ring, tilting it all over on its sides to cover the outer edges with chocolate. Turn over to run off the excess chocolate. Leave to set for a few minutes, then repeat until the chocolate is 3 cm (1¼ in) thick.

4. Turn over onto a baking sheet and smooth the edges. Turn the box over and after a few minutes, trim the edges using a triangular spatula. Leave the three parts of the box to set at room temperature, ideally 15–17°C (59–62°F) for 48 hours.

5. Unmould the base of the box, the lid and the handle.

6. Using a knife with a warm blade, cut the chocolate ring for the handle into 2 semi-circles.

7. Roughen the top of the lid and the handle carefully using the wire brush.

8. Gently brush the whole of the outside of the box using the wire brush.

9. Heat a baking tray on a double-boiler (page 118). Place the base of the semi-circular handle on the warmed tray for a few seconds to melt it slightly, then immediately fix it in place on the lid. Fill with chocolates of your choice.

CHOCOLATE FISH

*Dark, white or milk chocolate moulded shapes
traditionally representing small fish or shellfish.*

**DARK, WHITE OR
MILK CHOCOLATE**

HOW LONG WILL IT TAKE?

Preparation: 1 hour
Setting: 48 hours

EQUIPMENT YOU WILL NEED

Thermometer
Polycarbonate mould
Polyethylene sheet

SKILLS REQUIRED

Tempering chocolate (page 24)
Making moulded chocolates (page 34)

TRICKY POINT

Tempering the couverture chocolate

ADVICE

For a speckled effect, separately temper (page 24) 100 g (3½ oz) white couverture and 300 g (10½ oz) dark couverture. Using a dry brush, tap spots of white couverture into the mould. Wait a few minutes, scrape off any excess (page 113), then fill with dark couverture chocolate.

PLANNING AND PREP

2 days before: Tempering – moulding
On the day: Unmoulding

MAKES 300 G (10½ OZ) SMALL FISH

300 g (10 ½ oz) dark, milk or
white couverture chocolate

1. Temper (page 24) the couverture
chocolate of your choice.

2. Using a dry brush, tap some couverture
into the bottom of the mould inserts, wait
a few minutes, then scrape off any excess.

3. Fill up the mould with the couverture

chocolate, tapping the side of the
mould with the handle of a spatula
to remove any air bubbles.

4. Scrape off excess chocolate using a
spatula. Place a polyethylene sheet on top
and use the spatula to smooth the top.

5. Leave to set at room temperature,
ideally 15–17°C (59–62°F) for 48 hours.
After setting, remove from the mould.

CHOCOLATE SLABS

*Slabs of dark, white or milk chocolate, covered
with dried and crystallised (candied) fruit.*

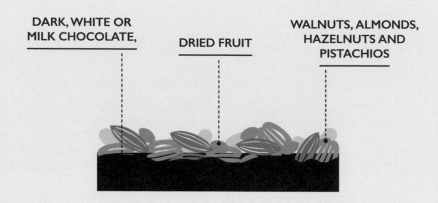

**DARK, WHITE OR
MILK CHOCOLATE,**

DRIED FRUIT

**WALNUTS, ALMONDS,
HAZELNUTS AND
PISTACHIOS**

HOW LONG WILL IT TAKE?

Preparation: 1 hour
Cooking: 20 minutes
Setting: 48 hours

EQUIPMENT YOU WILL NEED

15 × 15 cm (6½ × 6½ in) baking frame
Thermometer
Polyethylene sheet

TRICKY POINT

Tempering the couverture chocolate

SKILLS REQUIRED

Roasting (page 125)
Tempering chocolate (page 24)

TIP

If you don't have a polyethylene
sheet, use baking parchment.

PLANNING AND PREP

On the day: Tempering – making – setting
2 days later: Ready to enjoy

MAKES 1 SLAB OF DARK, WHITE OR MILK CHOCOLATE

MILK CHOCOLATE

30 g (1 oz) whole blanched hazelnuts
30 g (1 oz) whole blanched almonds
30 g (1 oz) shelled walnut halves
30 g (1 oz) whole shelled pistachios
300 g (10½ oz) milk couverture chocolate

DARK CHOCOLATE

30 g (1 oz) crystallised (candied) lemon
40 g (1½ oz) dried cranberries
20 g (½ oz) dried bananas
300 g (10½ oz) dark couverture chocolate (66% cocoa)
30 g (1 oz) puffed rice

WHITE CHOCOLATE

10 g (½ oz) dried strawberries
15 g (½ oz) dried blueberries
30 g (1 oz) roasted cashews
10 g (½ oz) dried goji berries
15 g (½ oz) dried cranberries
300 g (10½ oz) white couverture chocolate

1. Roast the nuts (page 125) for 20 minutes at 160°C (320°F/gas 4), then leave to cool. Cut the crystallised fruit into 1 cm (½ in) wide sticks. Temper your chosen chocolate (page 24).

2. For the slab of dark chocolate, stir the puffed rice into the chocolate couverture before pouring.

3. Place the baking frame on the polyethylene sheet and pour the chocolate in a uniform layer. Add the dried and candied fruit immediately, pushing it slightly into the surface. Leave to set at room temperature, ideally 15–17°C (59–62°F) for 48 hours.

4. After setting, break into pieces by dropping the slab onto the work surface, or by using a knife or mallet. It's ready for you to enjoy.

MENDIANTS

Dark chocolate discs covered with dried and candied fruit.

DARK CHOCOLATE **CANDIED FRUIT** **DRIED FRUIT AND NUTS**

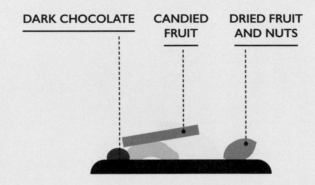

HOW LONG WILL IT TAKE?

Preparation: 1 hour
Cooking: 20 min
Standing: 48 hours (to crystallize)

EQUIPMENT YOU WILL NEED

Thermometer
Piping bag
Polyethylene sheet

VARIATION

Replace some of the dried fruit with pecans, goji berries or dried bananas.

TRICKY POINT

Tempering the couverture chocolate

SKILLS REQUIRED

Roasting (page 125)
Tempering chocolate (page 24)
Using a piping bag (page 120)

ADVICE

Avoid holding the piping bag in your hands for too long: body temperature is higher than the chocolate temperature, and the warming may cause the chocolate to develop a white 'bloom'.

TIP

If you don't have a polyethylene sheet, use baking parchment.

PLANNING AND PREP

On the day: Tempering – making – setting
2 days later: Ready to enjoy

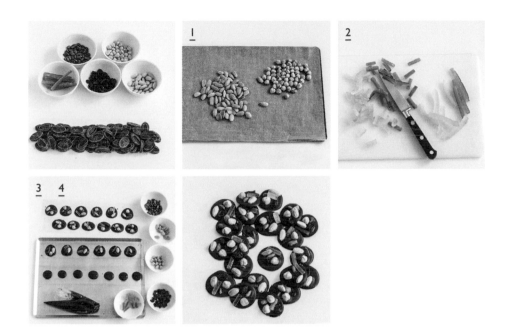

MAKES 40 MENDIANTS

30 g (1 oz) whole shelled almonds
30 g (1 oz) whole shelled hazelnuts
40 g (1 oz) crystallised (candied)
orange and lemon
300 g (10 ½ oz) dark couverture
chocolate (66% cocoa)
30 g (1 oz) cranberries
30 g (1 oz) pistachios

1. Roast the almonds and hazelnuts
(page 125) for 20 minutes at 160°C
(320°F/gas 4), then leave to cool.

2. Cut the crystallised oranges
into 1 cm (½ in) sticks.

3. Temper the couverture (page 24).

4. Transfer the couverture to a piping bag
and cut a small hole in a corner of the bag
(page 120). Pipe out a row of discs on the
polyethylene sheet: hold the piping bag
upright, squeeze the end between thumb
and forefinger to stop the flow, then without
moving the bag let the chocolate run out to
form a 2 cm (¾ in) diameter disc. Squeeze the
bag again to stop the flow, move the piping
bag along and repeat the process. At the end
of the row, put the bag down and tap the tray
to enlarge the discs to a diameter of 3–4 cm
(1 ¼–1 ½ in). Arrange the dried and crystallised
fruit neatly on top of the chocolate discs,
pressing it lightly into the surface.

5. Leave to set at room temperature,
ideally 15–17°C (59–62°F), for 48 hours.

ORANGETTES

Candied orange sticks coated with dark chocolate.

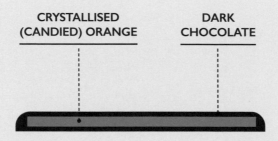

CRYSTALLISED (CANDIED) ORANGE

DARK CHOCOLATE

HOW LONG WILL IT TAKE?

Preparation: 1 hour 30 minutes
Setting: 48 hours

EQUIPMENT YOU WILL NEED

Thermometer
Dipping fork

VARIATION

Instead of crystallised orange use crystallised ginger, lemon or grapefruit. Crystallised lemon and grapefruit go well with milk chocolate couverture.

TRICKY POINTS

Tempering the couverture chocolate
Coating the chocolates

SKILLS REQUIRED

Tempering chocolate (page 24)
Coating with a dipping fork (page 32)

PLANNING AND PREP

On the day: Coating – setting
2 days later: Ready to enjoy

MAKES ABOUT 50

30 g (1 oz) potato starch
30 g (1 oz) icing (confectioner's) sugar
150 g (5 oz) crystallised orange sticks

COATING

300 g (10 ½ oz) dark couverture
chocolate (66% cocoa)

1. Mix the potato starch and icing sugar in a
bowl. Add the crystallised orange sticks
and coat well. Sieve to remove the excess.

2. Temper the coating couverture (page 24).

3. Dip the sticks into the chocolate one
by one, making up-and-down movements
with each stick to thoroughly coat.
The chocolate should cling to the fruit
and not run off the stick. Scrape the
fork over the rim to remove the excess
chocolate, then transfer it to the sheet.

4. Leave to set at a temperature of
15–17°C (59–62°F) for 48 hours.

CHOCOLATE BARS

Crispy bar covered with milk ganache and redcurrant
jelly and coated with dark chocolate.

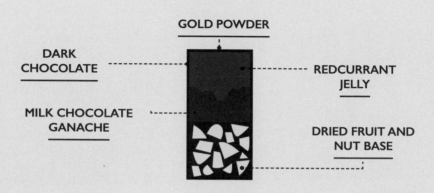

GOLD POWDER

DARK
CHOCOLATE

REDCURRANT
JELLY

MILK CHOCOLATE
GANACHE

DRIED FRUIT AND
NUT BASE

HOW LONG WILL IT TAKE?

Preparation: 3 hours
Cooking: 20 minutes
Standing: 12 hours (ganache)
Setting: 4 hours (jelly), plus 48 hours (bar)

EQUIPMENT YOU WILL NEED

16 × 16 cm (6½ × 6½ in) baking frame
Thermometer
Polyethylene sheets
Piping bag

VARIATIONS

Vary the fruit according to taste by replacing
redcurrant with raspberry or passion fruit

SKILLS REQUIRED

Roasting (page 125)
Tempering (page 24)
Rehydrating gelatine (page 119)
Coating with a thin layer of
chocolate (chabloning; page 115)
Using a piping bag (page 120)
Decorating with gold (page 125)

PLANNING, PREP AND STORAGE

4 days before: Crispy base – ganache
3 days before: Jelly
The day before: Coating – setting

The bars will keep for 1 week in an
airtight box at room temperature.

MAKES 10 BARS

CRISPY BASE

40 g (1½ oz) almonds, chopped
25 g (1 oz) macadamia nuts, crushed
100 g (3½ oz) dark chocolate (66% cocoa)
8 g (¼ oz) cocoa butter
15 g (½ oz) pumpkin seeds
15 g (½ oz) dried blueberries

MILK GANACHE

75 g (2½ oz) whipping cream
20 g (¾ oz) unsalted butter
25 g (1 oz) inverted sugar or neutral honey
100 g (3½ oz) milk chocolate

REDCURRANT JELLY

4 g (2 sheets) sheet gelatine
25 g (1 oz) white caster (superfine) sugar
6 g (¼ oz) powdered pectin
250 g (9 oz) redcurrant purée
20 g (¾ oz) inverted sugar or neutral honey

COATING AND FINISHING

600 g (1 lb 5 oz) dark couverture
chocolate (66% cocoa)
Gold powder

1. Place the baking frame on the
polyethylene sheet. To make the crispy base:
roast the almonds and crushed macadamia
nuts for 20 minutes at 160°C (320°F/gas
4). Melt the chocolate and cocoa butter
in a double-boiler (page 118). Away from
the double-boiler, add the pumpkin seeds,
dried blueberries, almonds and macadamia
nuts. Mix and spread on the polyethylene
sheet. Level the surface using a spatula.

2. To make the milk ganache: boil the
cream, butter and inverted sugar/honey.
Pour over the chocolate, wait 1 minute,
then stir. Mix, taking care to incorporate
as little air as possible (page 118). Cover
with cling film (plastic wrap) and set aside.
When the ganache is at 32°C (89.6°F),
spread it over the crispy base using a
spatula. Leave to set (page 25) for 12 hours.

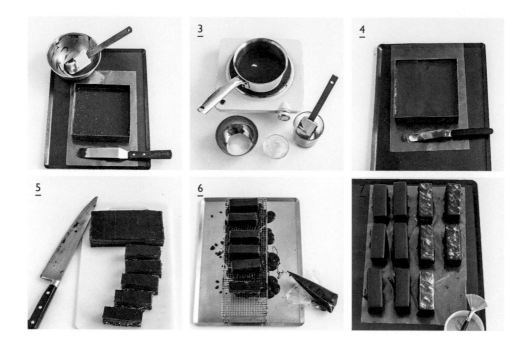

3. To make the redcurrant jelly: rehydrate the gelatine in cold water (page 119). Mix the sugar and pectin. Bring the redcurrant purée and inverted sugar/honey to the boil in a saucepan. Add the sugar-pectin mixture and cook for 1 minute, whisking all the time. Add the gelatine, stir, then transfer to a bowl and cover with cling film (plastic wrap).

4. When the jelly is at around 28°C (82°F), whisk it well to make it smooth, then spread it over the ganache layer using a palette knife. Transfer to the refrigerator to set for at least 4 hours. Remove any traces of condensation using paper towels.

5. Temper the coating couverture (page 24), then use a brush to coat the jelly layer with a thin layer of chocolate. Before the chocolate layer hardens, cut out 8 × 3 cm (3 × 1 in) rectangles using a chef's knife.

6. Put the rectangles on a rack set over a baking tray, spacing them out. Make a small hole in a piping bag and pipe the remaining chocolate out onto each bar. Gently shake the rack to allow excess chocolate to run off.

7. Place the chocolate bars on a tray lined with another polyethylene sheet. Using a dry brush, decorate with gold powder (page 125). Leave to set at room temperature, ideally 15–17°C (59–62°F), for 48 hours.

CHAPTER 3

ILLUSTRATED GLOSSARY

UTENSILS

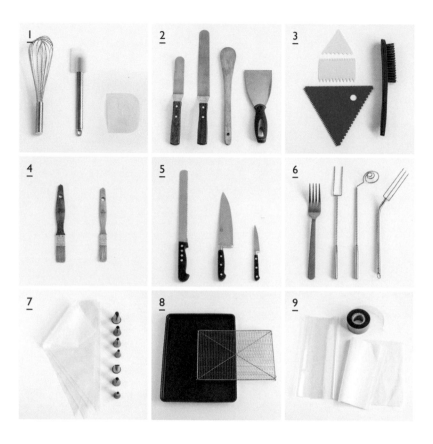

1. Whisk, rubber spatula, bowl scraper

2. Palette knives, spatulas

3. Comb spatulas, brush

4. Paint brushes

5. Serrated knife, chef's knife, paring knife

6. Fork, dipping forks

7. Piping bags, nozzles

8. Baking tray (pan), baking rack

9. Baking parchment, transparent acetate tape, polyethylene sheets

UTENSILS

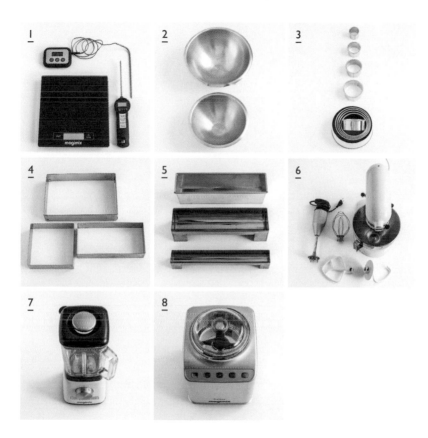

1. Scales, thermometers

2. Round bowls

3. Rings, pastry cutters

4. Baking frames

5. Log cake moulds/tins

6. Hand blender, stand mixer, attachments

7. Blender

8. Ice cream maker

CHOCOLATE MOULDS

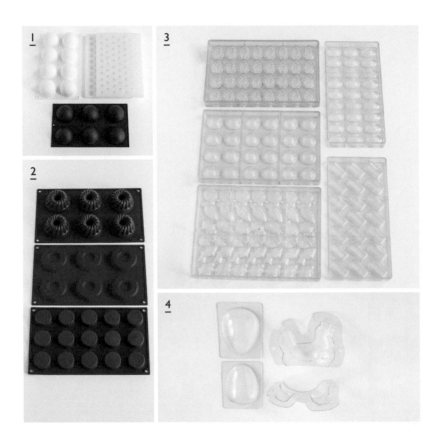

1. Half-sphere silicone moulds

2. Silicone moulds for babas, savarin moulds, discs

3. Chocolate moulds of various shapes, polycarbonate mould with small fish imprints

4. Polycarbonate moulds to make eggs and hens

CHOCOLATE MOULDS

1. KEEPING MOULDS CLEAN AND DRY

Wipe the mould imprints with a clean cloth before pouring the chocolate in to remove any trace of moisture or fat. Hold moulds by their edges to limit hand contact. Body heat is higher than the temperature at which chocolate is processed, and the heat may cause white "bloom" on the chocolate after setting.

2. FILLING A MOULD

Fill the mould with chocolate, tap lightly on the side to allow air bubbles to escape, then turn it over to let the excess chocolate flow out. Wait a few minutes, then repeat the operation.

3. SCRAPING

When the chocolate has begun to set, run a palette knife over the surface of the mould to remove excess chocolate and make sweets with neat, smooth edges

4. UNMOULDING

Twist the mould slightly, turn it over and tap the side with the handle of a spatula.

5. JOINING TWO CHOCOLATE PIECES TOGETHER

Heat a baking tray on a double-boiler, put the first piece on the tray for a few seconds so that it melts slightly and then stick it immediately to the second piece. Leave to crystallise.

CHOCOLATE PRODUCTS

WHITE/MILK/BLOND (CARAMELISED WHITE) CHOCOLATE

DARK CHOCOLATE (60%, 66%, 70%)

RAW CHOCOLATE

The cocoa beans for 'raw' chocolate bars have not been roasted. Avoiding heat treatment means that a maximum quantity of natural ingredients has been preserved. Its nutritional quality is superior to more processed chocolate.

COCOA BUTTER

Vegetable fat from the cocoa bean, used to make the chocolate more fluid when it is tempered and to give the tempered mixture more body.

MYCRYO BUTTER

Pure vegetable fat from the cocoa bean. This butter has a completely neutral taste.

COCOA POWDER

Unsweetened chocolate powder.

COCOA NIBS

Roasted and crushed cocoa beans, with a strong and rather bitter taste. They are used to add flavour and crunchiness.

COUVERTURE CHOCOLATE

Couverture chocolate is high-quality dark, white or milk chocolate packed in slabs, discs or chips and used by professional chocolatiers, chocolate-makers and pastry chefs. Bars of dark, milk or white chocolate come in 70 g (2½ oz) to 100 g (3½ oz) bars or individual squares. Couverture chocolate is chosen when the product will be melted and processed. It contains less sugar and more cocoa butter (31% minimum). When melted, it is more fluid and creamy and coats well. It has a good consistency when tempered. Bars of eating chocolate may also be used for making decorations that do not require melting.

A CHOCOLATE GLOSSARY

COATING WITH A THIN LAYER OF CHOCOLATE

Called 'chabloning' in French. Applying a fine layer of melted chocolate on a biscuit base, which hardens as it dries.
Use regular baking chocolate, which does not require tempering. Melt it in a double-boiler, pour it over the biscuit base and spread as thinly as possible using a palette knife. Leave to harden. When assembling, place chocolate-side down.

TEMPERING

The process by which the fat contained in the chocolate changes from a liquid to a solid state. Once solid, the fat molecules interlock with each other, giving them rigidity and hardness.
Cocoa butter (the fat in the chocolate) is made up of mainly triglycerides which, depending on the temperature at which tempering takes place, can have up to five different crystal forms, each of which is stable at a particular temperature. The process of tempering is crucial for giving chocolate its lovely sheen and texture that breaks with a snap.

TEMPERATURE CURVES
Dark couverture chocolate:
Melting temp: 55–58°C (131–136.4°F) / Tempering temp: 28–29°C (82.4–84.2°F) / Working temp: 31–32°C (87.8–89.6°F).
Milk couverture chocolate:
Melting temp: 45–48°C (113–118.4°F) / Tempering temp: 27–28°C (80.6–82.4°F) / Working temp: 29–30°C (84.2–86°F).
White couverture chocolate:
Melting temp: 45–48°C (113–118.4F°) / Tempering temp: 26–27°C (78.8–80.6°F) / Working temp: 28–29°C (82.4–84.2°F).

REMOVING A BAKING FRAME

Gently heat the outside of the frame using a kitchen blowtorch or run the hot blade of a knife between the ganache chocolate and the baking frame.

STRAINING GLAZE

Strain the chocolate glaze through a fine sieve in order to remove any impurities from the ingredients.

TIPS: MAKING CHOCOLATE

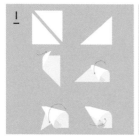   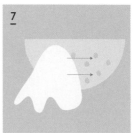

1. MAKING A PAPER CONE FOR PIPING

Cut out a 30 × 20 cm (12 × 8 in) right-angled triangle from a sheet of baking parchment. Holding the 30 cm (12 in) base in the middle and with the right angle on your right, bring down the tip opposite the middle of the base and start rounding the cone, turning it on itself until you reach the opposite tip. Bend the opposite point into the cone to hold it in position. Make sure that the tip of the cone is sharp. Fill the cone one-third full with the piping mixture, fold down the tip like a tube of toothpaste and cut off the tip to the required size.

2. TEMPERATURE

Use an accurate thermometer, ideally displaying one digit after the decimal point, to make sure that a dark couverture chocolate, for example, is between 31 and 32°C (87.8 and 89.6°F). To test the temperature, leave the thermometer in the middle of the mixture and stir until the temperature remains constant.

3. BLOOMED CHOCOLATE

There are several possible causes: moisture in the mould, cooling too quickly – this happens when you put the mould in the refrigerator – or incorrect tempering. Before using tempered couverture chocolate, dip a piece of baking parchment into the chocolate mixture and leave the coating to set on the worktop. If after a few minutes it hardens, breaks cleanly and does not melt instantly when touched, it can be used, otherwise you will need to start the process again.

4. THICKENED CHOCOLATE

If chocolate thickens during tempering, it will unfortunately never recover its fluid texture. It is best to set it aside and use for making ganache or mousse.

5. VISCOUS CHOCOLATE

If you let the temperature drop too far during tempering, the chocolate will begin to thicken and become viscous as it cools: unstable crystals have formed, having a negative effect on the texture of the chocolate.

CHOOSING CHOCOLATE

6. SHRINKAGE OF GANACHE

It is best to leave ganache to set for 1–2 hours to prevent shrinkage when it is moulded or used for coating. Shrinkage produces air gaps, making the chocolate difficult to keep long-term.

7. KEEPING EQUIPMENT CLEAN AND DRY

Clean and dry the bowl thoroughly each time you use the double-boiler. Avoid washing your hands while working with chocolate to prevent moisture from getting into the couverture chocolate. Moisture will make the surface rough (a process called 'seizing') and may later cause the chocolate to form a white 'bloom' on its surface.

BUYING CHOCOLATE

When buying chocolate you should check there is a minimum of 30% cocoa. In the UK and Europe, the term 'made from pure cocoa butter product' or '100% pure cocoa butter' guarantees that the finished product has no added vegetable oils other than cocoa butter. The word 'origin' followed by the name of the country, means that the beans are wholly from the producing country indicated.

Chocolate bearing the AB label complies with the European CE directive, which refers to the organic production of agricultural products without the use of chemicals such as pesticides. At least 95% of the ingredients must be organically produced. The cocoa beans, cocoa butter, sugar and other milk products used in the production of organic chocolate are from agriculture that complies with the European directive.

WHERE SHOULD YOU BUY CHOCOLATE?

Bean-to-bar chocolatiers: these are specialists in the craft of producing chocolate, buying beans directly from growers and processing and producing the chocolate end-to-end. Buy direct from the producer, from reliable shops and online.

Eating chocolate: bars of good-quality eating chocolate and baking chocolate are available from shops and supermarkets.

Couverture chocolate: can be bought in specialised professional shops or online, often in in 1kg (2.2 lb) to 3 kg (6.6 lb) bags.

HOW TO KEEP AND STORE

Chocolate should be kept out of the refrigerator away from light and heat. Put it in a dry place ideally between 16°C (60°F) and 18°C (64.5°F). Ganaches should be eaten within three weeks of when they're made, and bars of chocolate can be kept for up to six months.

BASIC TECHNIQUES: MAKING

1. INCORPORATING USING A SPATULA

Use a whisk to incorporate one third of the smoother, more runny mix into a second third in order to loosen it up. Then stir this mix into the remaining third using a spatula until you obtain a smooth, light mix.

2. MIXING WITHOUT INCORPORATING AIR

Push the stem of the mixer down to the bottom of the bowl and move it around gently in order to allow any air caught in the blades to escape, then mix without lifting.

3. SCRAPING

Scrape the sides of the bowl using a spatula or a bowl scraper to recover as much of the mixture as possible.

4. USING A DOUBLE-BOILER

The double-boiler makes it possible to heat ingredients, using steam, away from direct contact with a heat source. Because the heat is less intense, the mixture warms up and melts gently. This technique prevents burning chocolate or coagulating eggs. Use a large saucepan and a larger diameter bowl so that you can rest the bowl on the saucepan without the bottom coming into contact with the water. Put water in the saucepan and heat it up to simmer but not boil. Put the mixture in the bowl and the bowl on the saucepan. The base of the bowl must not touch the water.

5. STRAINING

Using a round or conical sieve with a more or less fine mesh makes a mixture more fluid and/or eliminates lumps.

BASIC TECHNIQUES: PREPARING

I. REHYDRATING GELATINE

These recipes are made using sheets of dehydrated gelatine (for best results do not use powdered gelatine). Because it is so light, gelatine must be weighed carefully before use. For precision, measurements are in grams in this book. One sheet of gelatine usually weighs 2 grams, but weights vary between brands. Gelatine must be rehydrated before it can be used for cooking. If it is not properly rehydrated, it will absorb further moisture from the mixture into which it is added and make it shrink. Immerse the gelatine in a large bowl of cold water (it melts at low temperature). Let it soak for at least 15 minutes. Squeeze out the gelatine between your hands before adding it to the mix using a whisk. Gelatine is used to help mixes stick together and give them body. Setting time is quite fast. Use the soaked gelatine as soon as possible so that the gelling power acts when the mixture is ready.

2. PREPARING A BAKING TRAY

Non-stick baking trays are available, but most trays must be lined with a non-stick surface: silicone cooking mats, baking parchment. Silicone mats are perfect for working with chocolate. Baking parchment is very handy, but less stable. Hold the corners in place with paper clips or put weights on top. Pipe out the mix then remove the weights when the piped mix is heavy enough to hold the parchment down by itself.

3. LINING A BAKING RING

Lightly butter the inside of the ring. Cut out a strip of baking parchment slightly higher than the side of the ring and 1 cm (½ in) longer in circumference. Put the strip in the ring and stick it to the sides before pouring in the mixture.

4. USING ACETATE STRIPS

Transparent acetate strip (Le Rhodoid is a brand name to look out for) is flexible and very useful for working with chocolate. Cut the strip so that it is slightly higher than the top of the ring or frame. Insert the strip into each ring, pour in the mixture and set in a cool place. The tape prevents desserts from sticking to the ring; it also makes unmoulding clean and easy and protects against oxidation.

5. SETTING UP FOR GLAZING

Put the item to be glazed on a wire rack placed on a rimmed baking tray. Pour on the glaze. Smooth out the top with a palette knife to remove any excess, which you can collect in the tray for further use.

BASIC TECHNIQUES: PIPING

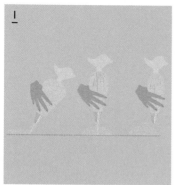
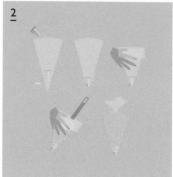
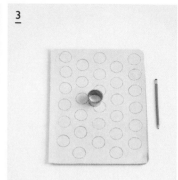

1. PIPING

A piping bag or pastry bag can be used without a nozzle to neatly fill a tart base or to make large round bases ensuring that the mixture is of even thickness. Fitted with a nozzle, the piping bag allows mixtures to be piped out very precisely or can give a special shape to the preparation.

Hold the piping bag upright to press out discs or domes, lay it horizontally to shape éclairs. Squeeze with one hand, stabilise and guide the piping bag with the other. When there is not enough mixture left in the section of bag in your hand, push the dough down and rotate the piping bag a quarter turn.

2. FILLING THE PIPING BAG

Select a nozzle and insert it into the piping bag. Mark off where to cut so that the socket fits properly. Remove the nozzle and cut the end off the bag. Twist the nozzle firmly down into the bottom of the piping bag to prevent the mixture from leaking out during filling. Fold out the top of the piping bag over the hand holding it. Using a spatula, transfer the dough or ganache into the piping bag, scraping the spatula on the hand holding the bag.

Fill the bag to a maximum of two-thirds full so that it does not overflow. Pull the top of the bag back up and give it a quarter turn to push the dough down towards the nozzle. Remove the cap from the nozzle and twist the piping bag to push out the dough or ganache.

3. MAKING A TEMPLATE

To ensure regular sizes when piping, use a template as a guide. Using a pencil, draw circles of the required size on a sheet of baking parchment. Turn it over and pipe out the mixture onto the drawn circles.

BASIC TECHNIQUES: FINISHING

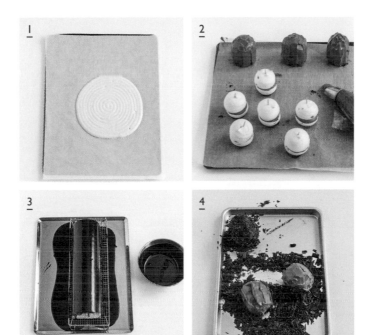

1. PIPING OUT A SPIRAL

Pipe out a mixture spiralling from the centre outwards and squeezing the piping bag with continuous, equal pressure to ensure a regular shape without gaps or overlapping between each spiral of mixture.

2. COATING USING A PIPING BAG

Coat the chocolate or cake using a piping bag fitted with a basket-weave nozzle.

3. GLAZING A LOG CAKE

Put the cake on a wire rack placed on a rimmed baking tray (pan). Pour out the glaze moving slowly from one end to the other. Gently shake the grid to remove excess glaze.

4. COVERING WITH FLAKES

Coat the chocolate using a piping bag, then roll it several times in the chocolate flakes.

INGREDIENTS: CREAM AND BUTTER

CREAM

1 THE PRODUCT

These recipes are made using fresh cream labelled 'whipping cream', which has a fat content of 36% (UK) or 35% (US). The cream used by French pâtissiers and chocolatiers has a similar fat content (30–34%). There are various types of cream: raw (unprocessed), pasteurised (heated to 80°C/176°F) or sterilised (processed at a very high temperature). It can come in liquid form or be thickened by adding lactic ferments. Pastry chefs and chocolate makers use cream with at least 30% fat because fat gives more body to the cream and adds taste. It is emulsified with melted chocolate to make ganaches, bringing smoothness and finesse.

2 MAKING WHIPPED CREAM

Whip the cream briskly until it doubles in volume. It becomes airy and firm as the fat globules in the cream enclose air and form bubbles. Use a food processor with a whisk, a cutter with a blade or an electric mixer.

3 FIRMING UP WHIPPED CREAM

To finish whipping up cream, increase the length and speed of movement to make it firm, smooth and evenly blended. The cream should lose some of its shininess.

BUTTER

4 THE PRODUCT

The butter used in these recipes is unsalted cow's milk butter. Use quality butter with a high percentage of fat (ideally around 82%), as this makes mixtures tasty, smooth and crumbly.

5 SOFTENED BUTTER

Softening butter before incorporating it into a mix helps prevent lumps forming and gives smoothness. Cut the butter into small pieces, let it soften at room temperature or soften it at very low heat (without melting it), then work it with a spatula or a whisk to a creamy consistency.

6 BROWNED 'HAZELNUT BUTTER'

Put the butter in a saucepan on a medium–low heat. When the crackling sound stops, the butter will have taken on a light hazelnut colour, as the casein (protein) in the butter caramelises and colours. Browned butter has a rich, toasty flavour.

THE INGREDIENTS: EGGS

EGGS

1 THE PRODUCT

Egg white contains proteins; egg yolk contains fat.

2 EQUIVALENT WEIGHTS

One fresh egg: 50 g (2 oz)
Egg white: 30–35g (1 oz)
Yolk: 15–20 g (¾ oz)

3 BEATING YOLKS

Whisk egg yolks and sugar to make a frothy mixture. It should double in volume. The process takes several minutes and is faster if you use an electric whisk.

4 WHIPPING AND FIRMING-UP EGG WHITES

Beat egg whites with a food processor with a whisk attachment or a hand mixer until they are firm and form peaks when the whisk is removed. Towards the end of whisking, increase the speed to make the whipped egg whites smooth and evenly blended. If necessary, add a little powdered sugar.

5 THE 'RIBBON TEST'

The consistency of a mixture of egg yolks, or egg whites, and sugar should be smooth and even so that it rolls off the spatula in a continuous stream without breaking, with a ribbon-like appearance.

INGREDIENTS: SUGAR AND HONEY

SUGAR

1 THE PRODUCT

Sugar enhances aromas, gives crispness, nourishes the yeast in leavened doughs and adds colour to baked cakes.

White caster sugar: refined powdered sugar, traditionally used in pastry making.

Icing (confectioner's) sugar: white sugar powder finely ground and enriched with starch to prevent solidification.

Brown sugar: raw sugar extracted from sugar cane.

Barbados: sugar made from the residual syrup from the refining of cane sugar.

2 MAKING A SYRUP

Use clean, dry utensils. Weigh the water and sugar, then pour them gently without mixing. Clean off any splashes using a water-soaked paintbrush. Heat over medium heat keeping an eye on the saucepan.

3 MAKING CARAMEL

Traditional caramel is made from sugar and water for sugar decorations. Dry caramel is made without water for the flavouring of mixtures that require a stronger taste.

4 SOAKING WITH SYRUP

Dip the paintbrush in the syrup and paint it on the biscuit base until it is fully soaked but not soggy. When you press down on the biscuit with your finger, the syrup should appear on the surface.

5. HONEY

A natural product from the beehive, bees' honey has a characteristic taste and is a powerful sweetener.

6. INVERTED SUGAR SYRUP

A mixture of glucose and fructose in equal proportions. It replaces sugar in some recipes because it has the characteristic of remaining soft and smooth without crystallising. Buy from specialist baking shops or online. If unavailable, use a neutral honey instead.

7. GLUCOSE SYRUP

A thick, colourless starch-based syrup made from corn or potato starch. It avoids the problem of crystallisation of sugar during cooking and is particularly used in glazes.

INGREDIENTS: FRUIT AND FLAVOURINGS

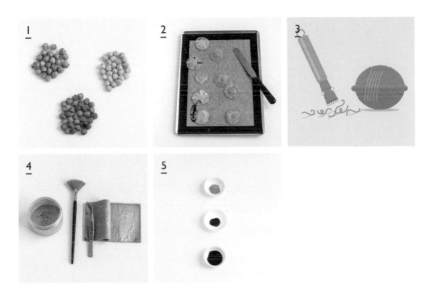

1. ROASTING DRIED NUTS

Place them on a baking sheet lined with baking parchment. Bake at 170°C (340°F/gas 5) for 15–25 minutes depending on their size. Roasting develops their aromas.

2. DRYING FRUIT

Cut thin slices of fruit. Preheat the oven to 90°C (200°F/gas ¼). Place the slices on a silicone cooking sheet and dry in the oven for 1½–2 hours, turning them over halfway through, keeping an eye on them all the time.

3. ZESTING FRUIT

The coloured, visible part of citrus fruit with an intense tangy taste. The pith is the bitter white part between the pulp and the peel and should not be used.

4. GOLD DECORATIONS

Edible gold for decorating food comes in powder, flakes or leaves. It is applied with a paintbrush and does not have any particular taste but has a very fine, decorative effect.

5. FOOD COLOURING

These recipes use fat-soluble colouring powders. These should generally be mixed with white couverture chocolate at two 3-minute intervals to obtain the right shade of colour.

INGREDIENT INDEX

First published in 2019 by Hachette Livre (Marabout)
This English language edition published in 2023 by Hardie
Grant Books, an imprint of Hardie Grant Publishing

Hardie Grant Books (London)
5th & 6th Floors
52–54 Southwark Street
London SE1 1UN

Hardie Grant Books (Melbourne)
Building 1, 658 Church Street
Richmond, Victoria 3121

hardiegrantbooks.com

The Little Book of Chocolate: Sweet Treats

ISBN: 978-1-78488-596-0

10 9 8 7 6 5 4 3 2 1

For the French edition:
Author: Mélanie Dupuis
Photography: Pierre Javelle
Illustrator: Yannis Varoutsikos

For the English edition:
Publisher: Kajal Mistry
Commissioning Editor: Eve Marleau
Editor: Isabel Gonzalez-Prendergast
Designer: Hart Studio
Proofreader: Claire Rogers
Production Controller: Martina Georgieva
Colour reproduction by p2d
Printed and bound in China by Leo Paper Products Ltd.